FORTUNE
TELLER'S
DICTIONARY

FORTUNE TELLER'S
DICTIONARY

EVERYTHING YOU NEED TO
KNOW ABOUT THE WORLD OF
FORTUNE-TELLING

COMPREHENSIVE EXPLANATIONS
OF PSYCHIC POTENTIAL,
INTUITION DEVELOPMENT,
AND DIVINATION PRACTICES

Antonia Beattie

THUNDER BAY
P · R · E · S · S
SAN DIEGO, CALIFORNIA

For I dipped into the future,
far as human eye could see,
Saw the vision of the world,
and all the wonder that would be ...

TENNYSON

CONTENTS

INTRODUCTION

There are many aspects to fortune-telling and there are many techniques that will help you tap into the future. Some are easily learned and can be practiced at home; others are more advanced methods, and require long-term, in-depth study and a consultation with a reputable and experienced person of the chosen craft.

This Dictionary will teach you the do-it-yourself practices of fortune-telling, plus give you insight into the more advanced methods. You may soon have a favorite craft, or you may prefer to indulge in all the elementary methods. Whatever your personal choice, you may be sure that in taking the time to study the easy lessons in the following pages, you will have opened the door to psychic awareness, as well as mastering a number of crafts which will bring you pleasure.

Imagine, for example, the pleasant surprise your dinner guests will get when they discover that you are able to entertain them with your newfound skills. Fortune-telling is an enjoyable pastime which few people can resist. The only problem these practices will leave you with is persuading your guests to leave!

You will have fun selecting a new baby's name, or finding your lucky numbers with the help of numerology, or discovering how many children you will have by reading the palms of your hands. And a pleasant cup of tea or coffee becomes something completely different when it is followed by a reading of the tealeaves or coffee grounds.

Whether we choose to believe that life is what we make it or that everything is predestined and therefore cannot be changed, curiosity compels us to seek all the help we can get with the important choices and decisions we must make throughout life.

Fortune-telling has long been a favorite way for a great many people seeking direction on such important issues as love, finance, health, and career. In this age of new awareness about psychic power, the multiple benefits of such knowledge become increasingly obvious.

We are all motivated to develop our powers of perception and intuition, recognizing their quality and value as we strive to achieve our personal goals. Our mental powers, such as intuition, are heightened during the process of psychic development, and this gives us greater power over our own destiny.

Poor choices in personal relationships can have a devastating impact on your life, with long-term side effects. How many times have you had to ask yourself, "Why didn't I listen to my intuition?"—once the damage has been done? Psychic development trains you to listen to and respect your intuition. How much easier it would be to make the right decisions and choices, in advance, about important aspects of your life—you can, if you are armed with advanced intuitive instinct.

The exercises and meditation formulas described in this book are designed to aid you in your psychic development. They are precise and easy to comprehend. You will discover how to increase your telepathic skills, and you will develop skills in clairvoyance, cards, psychometry, and palmistry.

You will learn the advantages of meditation, such as how to relax the body and mind, and how to focus, and you will also become aware of the importance of protecting yourself from negative influences.

You will discover the fine line between coincidence, intuition, and psychic phenomena, and how they all relate to your innate psychic ability. This Dictionary will also explain to you the importance of knowing when it is appropriate to use your psychic ability and when it is not.

Above all else, this Dictionary will help you enjoy discovering your own unique path toward spiritual enlightenment.

YOUR PSYCHIC ABILITY

What Is Psychic Ability?

To understand the notion of psychic phenomena you need to realize that the mind is a powerful vehicle of communication. It requires its operator to make use of its full potential, and this operator must always be you.

Many notable events are attributed to coincidence, but is it really your intuition at work? Things happen simply by chance, or so it seems, but in many of these instances our instincts have propelled us to be in a certain place at a certain time, or have detained or prevented us from being somewhere we had intended to be.

The result of these coincidences can be profound: for instance, how often have you heard someone sigh with relief because some unexpected circumstance caused them to miss a journey that ended in disaster?

Then there are those people whose lives have been changed—career paths, lovers, bank balances—simply because they happened to be in the right place at the right time. Some might say that these occurrences are coincidence. But sometimes these events are just too strange and too significant to be dismissed so easily.

Apparent coincidences happen all the time. For instance, have you ever gone into a bookstore looking for a book on a particular subject, and while you were wandering the aisles, a book on a completely unrelated subject either fell from the shelf in front of you or was brought to your attention in an equally unusual way? It turns out that this book provides answers to a dilemma you were facing or benefits you in some other way that matters.

Those who are able to accurately predict world events or see into the secrets and intimate experiences of people they have never met or even seen before are referred to as psychics—a collective term describing people who can see, hear, or feel significant incidents with clarity, either through advanced psychic awareness or with the aid of a medium such as tarot cards, a crystal ball, tea-leaf or coffee ground readings, or other devices.

By developing your own psychic ability you will discover which of these disciplines most suits you; this will be the one you will go on to perfect.

Few people embark on a journey of exploration into the unknown without knowledge of its advantages and disadvantages. All knowledge is not necessarily good knowledge, but all good knowledge should be valued. Psychic development delivers valuable knowledge about reaching your full potential in both spiritual and material development.

Psychic messages come in many forms; coincidence is just one of them. Dreams, papers being blown off a desk that reveal something to you, items being knocked over and drawing your attention to something are just a few of the ways that a psychic message might come to you. Any of these could be your guardian angel trying to get a message through to you.

When all your senses, including your sixth sense—intuition or, in its more powerful form, ESP (extrasensory perception)—are working to their fullest capacity, there will be little you cannot achieve through effort and commitment to the task at hand.

There will be fewer dangers to encounter because you are now able to sense negative energy in people and places. In your personal relationships, you will be less likely to choose a wrong mate, for you will now listen to that little voice that tells you someone is no good for you. Although it is commendable to base important career choices on practical and logical reasons, also take into account what your intuition is trying to tell you. Consider not taking a job if your intuition warns you that something is wrong.

Early Stages of Psychic Awareness

A re you psychic? Everyone interested in psychic phenomena wonders if they are psychic. Almost everybody has the potential to increase their psychic ability. The exceptions are those who fear its power and therefore reject it, and those who refuse to acknowledge its existence.

People with psychic ability have always been around—in tribal societies, advanced ancient civilizations, and our own highly technical world. Intuition, ESP, telepathy, clairvoyance, clairaudience, spiritualism, psychic healing, card reading, crystal gazing, and tea-leaf reading, among other skills, are individual or group disciplines that all come under the umbrella of psychic phenomena and skills. You can learn any one of these, or all of them, if you have the desire and the patience.

How many times have you known who is calling you when the phone rings? Have you ever woken from a deep sleep or stopped in your tracks, alarmed because you felt a loved one was in danger? If any of these things have happened to you, you have the potential for psychic development.

The following chapters will show you many simple ways to test your psychic potential and your progress, but first of all you must believe in yourself and commit to the task you have set yourself. Of course there are people who seem to be born with a highly developed psychic ability; most of those go on to become very useful to other people in all aspects of their lives.

People who see, hear, or feel impressions concerning events and circumstances of which they have no previous knowledge are known as psychics. If this is who you wish to be, much of your time and energy should be devoted to the study of psychic ability and to psychic-enhancing exercises.

Exploration of personal psychic ability in the early stages of awareness requires only simple detective exercises. Sometimes psychics are referred to as "sensitives." This term stems from the belief that in some degree or another we are all sensitive to the energy fields around us. Have you ever felt a distinct chill in the air while you have been in a warm building? Unlike the chill you feel when you are running a fever, a psychic chill is usually accompanied by an eerie feeling that disappears once you leave the scene.

There is another common psychic occurrence: sensing negative energies around you. This energy comes from people known as "psychic leeches" or "vampires." Is there someone in your life who demands a great deal from you? Do you feel drained and weak after a lengthy session with this person? If the answers to these questions are "yes," you have a problem.

Psychic leeches suck the energy from other people's auras without even being aware that they are doing so. If you are plagued in this manner, it is important to ask yourself if you are really doing this person any good by spending time trying to help them. There are two solutions to this situation. You can ask your guardian angel to put a shield of protection around you, or you can encourage that person not to be so reliant on you.

When you feel that you are picking up energies from the atmosphere, record these impressions—as they happen, if possible. This exercise not only strengthens your faith in your psychic ability, it will actually sharpen it as well.

Combining ESP with the sense of touch is an excellent way to practice and develop psychic ability. It could also lead to developing skills in the area of psychic healing. Naturally, these skills are not supposed to compete with those of orthodox medicine; they are a way you can help yourself heal, with your doctor's approval.

Dealing with the Psychic

Fear is the number one setback to any form or degree of psychic ability. Normally fear is an emotional force, and it should be respected in times of danger. However, it must be controlled, and it should never totally govern our decisions, choices, and actions.

To fear something or someone because you do not fully understand the concept or person is negative and self-destructive. This kind of fear can become a phobia if you imagine that some superior force will prevent or destroy your personal goals. To fear a tyrannical personality is understandable; but even a tyrant can intimidate you only for as long as you allow him or her to do so.

Fear originates from a lack of belief and confidence in yourself. There is a special exhilaration to overcoming your fear. However, before taking on a task that makes you fearful, gather as much information and protection as you need so that you can complete the task with as much help and safety as possible.

The main cause of failure to commit to psychic development is fear of the unknown. This must be overcome if you are ever to reach your full psychic potential. Fear of the unknown is similar in nature to fear of failure to succeed in relationships or business, and it too can prevent you from enjoying success. To fear the unknown is to rob your spirit of knowledge, which is the reward that comes with any new experience.

Superstitious fear is common. The list of superstitions is endless, some examples being: walking under a ladder, lucky number seven, Friday the thirteenth, shoes on a tabletop, and traveling without a lucky charm or talisman. While it is often treated in a lighthearted manner, superstitious fear does control the activities of many people. The mystery surrounding psychic phenomena attracts even those most fearful of its power. The best cure for fear of the unknown is knowledge.

When dealing with a psychic child, it is important not to fear, disapprove of, or ridicule the child for his or her psychic abilities. If you do this, the child will tend to become secretive, withdrawn, and shrouded by guilt, until he or she is drawn to another psychic person who understands his or her talent. The fact is, no matter how hard a parent might strive to suppress this tendency, it cannot be destroyed.

Samantha was fifteen years old before she sought the advice of a professional psychic to help her deal with her own psychic ability. She had been feeling so bad that she just wanted the psychic to make it all go away. Samantha had been having psychic experiences since she was seven years old, but the last five to six years had not been happy ones.

During the early years of her psychic experiences, Samantha had no problems with her ability to predict the future and talk to spirits whom she could see with clarity. The trouble began when her father became convinced that she was hallucinating as the result of mental problems. Her mother believed that an evil spirit possessed her daughter.

In their misguided effort to protect their daughter from ridicule and from being labeled insane, Samantha's parents took her to doctors and priests and finally to a psychotherapist. Her attitude to all these people was extremely bad, and coupled with her now restless mood swings, these actions resulted in Samantha's becoming very depressed and out of control.

Finally, on the advice of a friend, she consulted a psychic, who managed to make her understand that what was happening to her was not a bad thing, just unusual and special, the manifestation of her highly developed psychic ability. Once she had come to terms with this knowledge, Samantha was able to cope with her special gift; she is now a well-adjusted and happy young woman.

Seeing into the Future

CLAIRVOYANCE AND CLAIRAUDIENCE

Each of us has a valid interest in our destiny, and even when we fear it, curiosity compels us to seek answers to important questions concerning our future. We live on a material planet, so we need to know the answers to practical, materialistic questions. We are also curious about what happens when we die. Where do we go? Will we ever see our deceased loved ones again? There are so many questions. And so we find ourselves consulting a clairvoyant or a clairaudient who may have some of these answers.

Clairvoyants have the ability to see mentally that which is invisible to most, such as people, places, and events that have passed or are yet to occur. This ability is considered a gift and is a very advanced method of fortune-telling. Most people assume that all clairvoyants enlist the aid of tarot cards or a crystal ball to predict the future. While this is true of some, other clairvoyants do not need any aids whatsoever.

If clairvoyance becomes your specialty, you will need to acquire a descriptive vocabulary in order to relate your visual experiences in a manner that can be believed and understood by your client.

You should report exactly what you see; do not presume to fill in the blanks of a sketchy visual experience. When you attempt to do so, you may be changing the whole concept of the message behind the pictures you are seeing. You are just a messenger who is given information on a strictly "need to know" basis. And even though the sketchy pictures you see make no sense at all to you personally, they will make perfect sense to your client. This person has the other pieces of the puzzle.

Clairaudience is the ability to hear that which is inaudible to the majority of people. Clairaudients are believed to have the ability to

---

FORTUNE-TELLER'S TIP

It is an impossible task to prove that the information given by clairvoyants and clairaudients is genuine. However, information they have given a client about his or her past is often recognized as true, and predictions for the future often prove themselves.

communicate with the dead, with guardian angels, and sometimes with other entities from the spirit world. Being a clairaudient means that you have the supernatural power to hear words, sentences, or names transmitted from the spirit world.

Sometimes the words are loud and clear, but often they are muffled sounds that take intense concentration and patience to interpret. The supposed reason for this diversity is that the spirit who is attempting to catch your attention is not fully acquainted with this system of psychic communication.

Many clairaudients are unjustly branded fraudulent for their repeated attempts to sound out, aloud, exactly what they are hearing. Often a clairaudient asks the client a question such as: "Do you know someone whose name begins with a *ju* or a *chu?*" Most people believe that the psychic is guessing and looking to them for more information. But this is not the case.

When you consult with a psychic in this way, you open up a line of communication between the psychic and the spirit world. That line of communication becomes like a busy switchboard. You may be surprised how many souls would like to send you a message, and much like a poor telephone connection, the sound is muffled until the line is cleared. This may lead to an apparent miscommunication. Later a message that means nothing to the psychic may come through; however, it will make a great deal of sense to you.

If you decide clairaudience is going to be your specialty, you will find that with time and practice you will have less difficulty understanding the messages that are being transmitted to you. Once you have reached this stage of development your client will understand more clearly his or her deceased loved one's message.

PSYCHOMETRY

Psychometry is the art of fortune-telling by way of holding an object such as jewelry or clothing belonging to a person and meditating on the object until you see, feel, or hear past, present, or future events connected to the object's owner. While much time and practice are required to reach an advanced stage with this method of fortune-telling, basic psychometry is relatively easy to learn.

Elementary psychometry requires you to note the fragmented impressions that you receive about an object. Although these first impressions will not always make sense at the time, progress and hindsight will provide clarification.

It is important to make a note of all the impressions you receive. For instance, did you feel happy, sad, excited, or indifferent when you first handled the piece of jewelry? Did you experience a feeling of harmony, irritability, security, or instability? Little things mean a lot more than you may think in these early stages.

To start, make a mental note of your first impressions when you next shake hands with someone, and of the feeling you have when you next enter a person's home or a strange building. Before long, you will find yourself carrying out these checks automatically.

Be careful not to upset or offend anyone with your predictions, even when you become experienced enough to be able to make them. If you have nothing positive to report, don't report anything.

There are times when even the most celebrated psychometrists appear to have received mixed messages, resulting in confusion for their clients. If you are the client, and this happens to you, don't be afraid to explain to the psychometrist that some of the information seems relevant but some information cannot possibly relate to you.

There is usually a simple explanation for this mix-up. Items of jewelry that have been owned by other people will still emit vibrations relating to their former owners' destinies. Vibrations coming from such a piece could also reflect its former owner's present condition in the afterlife.

When Not to Use Your Psychic Talents

Sometimes, when you are using your psychic ability to predict the future for someone, you will have an impression of a terrible situation occurring in the future—the person may be a victim of accident, crime, natural disaster, or a fatal disease—and will wonder whether or not you should deliver the message. It is both unwise and irresponsible to pass on these sorts of predictions.

Only pass on predictions that are positive or can reverse an unhappy situation. To begin with, no psychic, no matter how experienced, can claim 100 percent accuracy—so it is possible for you to misinterpret the prediction. But more important, imagine how you would feel if a psychic told you that you were going to become the victim of a violent attack from which you could not escape, or that a drunken driver was going to run you down.

However, if you happen to be doing a psychic reading for someone and you see that this person is going to get behind the wheel of a car while they are intoxicated, and you see the person being responsible for an accident, you must certainly tell the person about what you see.

You should not use your psychic ability in any way if you are intoxicated or under the influence of drugs, or when you are experiencing emotional upheaval or depression. You should not use your psychic skills to predict the future for people who are likely to become dependent on you to solve all their problems—psychic ability is supposed to help people help themselves.

When you do psychic readings for someone whose actions are regarded by you or society as inappropriate (or worse), you should never make judgments about those actions. Instead, suggest to the person that he or she try to understand the full ramifications of such behavior.

Psychic readings are highly confidential, and nothing should induce you to divulge the confidential information with which you have been entrusted.

Getting into a Meditative State

MEDITATION AND FORTUNE-TELLING

Fortune-tellers benefit greatly from regular meditation exercises. Psychic development is a natural by-product of regular meditation, and its importance in enhancing your fortune-telling skills cannot be underestimated. The more relaxed you are when you do a fortune-telling reading, the more accurate your reading will be.

The advantages of meditation skills are immeasurable—they are the key to opening up and sharpening all your senses, including your sixth sense, which, being the most elusive and mysterious of the senses, requires the calming, persuasive influence of peace that the practice of meditation creates.

People whose lives are not lived at a frenetic pace find it relatively easy to practice meditation, but people who have to cope with stress every day may need to take time out to learn this wonderful skill.

Meditation exercises can be practiced in the privacy of your own home or in a group meditation such as a psychic workshop. Group meditation can be very effective, because the positive peaceful energy generated by a collection of people far outweighs that generated by one person.

Various methods of meditation are practiced in psychic workshops. Most of these methods are positive and successful, but there are some groups, fortunately a minority, that favor drug-induced methods of meditation. These are most definitely not recommended.

Try out the basic meditation method described here and see if it suits you. First, find a quiet space where you will not be disturbed. Either lie down or sit comfortably with your back

straight. Let your hands rest with your palms open. When you are comfortable, follow the steps below to start your relaxation exercise.

1 Take four long, slow, deep breaths, allowing the breath to travel to any areas in your body where you sense tension or tightness. Imagine that breath dissolving the tension into nothingness.

2 Put your legs out directly in front of you, point your toes, and then tighten the muscles along the fronts and backs of your legs all the way to your buttocks. Hold the muscles tightly for 20 seconds and then allow them to relax.

3 Tighten the muscles in your stomach and buttocks at the same time. Hold them firmly for 20 seconds and then allow them to soften and relax.

4 Squeeze your shoulder blades together, pushing your elbows behind your body and feeling the tension in the middle of your upper back while expanding your chest. Hold for 20 seconds and then allow your back to relax.

5 Put your arms out directly in front of you, make fists with your hands, and tighten the muscles all the way up your arms to your shoulders. Push your arms away from your body while you round your shoulders a little until you feel a stretch along your upper back. Hold for 20 seconds and then allow your arms to relax, placing your hands back in your lap or by your sides.

6 Shrug your shoulders as high as you can. Rotate them forward slowly three times and then backward three times. Let them drop softly into a comfortable position.

7 Tilt your head to the left, allowing the weight of your head to increase the stretch along the right side of your neck a little. Hold for 10 to 20 seconds, then return to the starting position.

8 Tilt your head to the right side, again allowing the weight of your head to increase the stretch along the left side of your neck. Hold for 10 to 20 seconds, and then return to the starting position.

9 Frown, squeeze your eyes shut, and purse your lips as hard as you can. Hold for 10 seconds, then allow your facial muscles to soften and relax.

10 Take three more long, slow, deep breaths and imagine the breath dissolving any residual tension in your body. Feel the difference within your body and the heightened sense of relaxation.

A PROTECTIVE WHITE LIGHTING EXERCISE

This method of meditation is very simple—anyone can do it. It takes just a little practice and the observance of the following fundamental basics:

1 Focus on something—breath, object, mantra, or music.
2 Gently push all thoughts aside (see pages 22–23 if you find this difficult).
3 Let go of the expectations of what you think should happen in the meditation, and allow yourself to simply "be" in the meditation. Whatever happens is perfect for that time and place.

Whether you choose to sit, lie, or walk, always be aware of your posture—sit, lie, or stand with a straight back so that no part of your body is scrunched or folded. It is easy for your shoulders to become rounded while you meditate, so start off with good posture and check your posture occasionally during the meditation.

Before you begin to meditate, do the simple relaxation exercise outlined on pages 18–19. When you meditate, you actually open energy centers within your body, which sometimes makes you vulnerable to the energy around you. At the beginning of each meditation, it is good practice to invoke some form of self-protection, such as the following "white lighting" exercise.

You can also use this exercise when you first get out of bed in the morning or just before you do a fortune-telling session—it helps you connect with your higher self, which is part of the universal energy (the "white light"). This pure energy offers with it supreme guidance; it allows only the highest frequency of universal energy to come to you while it is being invoked. It deflects any negative energy around you, whether this energy comes from the people around you, the places you visit, or from within your own mind.

This exercise also helps you be more balanced when dealing with others throughout the day. It helps you become more centered and get in touch with calming and healing energies, especially if you are feeling a little emotionally unbalanced or if you have suffered some kind of mental or emotional trauma. You can also use this method when you know you have to deal with someone who is difficult. It will help you maintain a centered composure during the interaction and see the situation objectively rather than emotionally.

To start the exercise, imagine a brilliant white light way above your head. Picture a single beam of pure brightness coming down from this light into the crown, or top, of your head. As you breathe, see that light filling your body slowly, starting with your head and face. The light pours into your body, filling every single cell. Imagine it pouring into your arms, right to the very ends of your fingertips. Then see the light filling your torso, buttocks and then legs, pouring into your feet, all the way to the tips of your toes.

Then imagine the light exiting through the bottom of your feet, going deep into the earth and then back up again into your legs. See that light overflowing the top of your head and pouring down around the sides of your body until it forms a cocoon of pure brightness around your entire body, with every part of your body enclosed.

See yourself within this beam of pure white light, which comes from the heavens, and anchored deep in the earth. And feel the protection it offers. It deflects any negative energy and helps you retain your own energy without it "leaking."

MANAGING DISTRACTIONS

When you are doing a reading for a client, friend, or yourself, you
will find that you get the best results when you are in a meditative
state. Sometimes it is hard to maintain that state when doorbells
and telephones ring, dogs bark, or airplanes fly overhead.

Do not allow yourself to become irritated by these distractions,
because such feelings are totally unproductive. What you can do is
make arrangements to manage the distractions that are within your
control. Turn on the answering machine for the telephone or ask
those you live with to take messages for you. Hang a sign requesting
quiet on your door.

Sometimes you will find it difficult to focus on the reading at
hand because you cannot seem to quiet your mind. Many people
believe they can never meditate because their minds are constantly
active; after all, we are blessed with intelligence and the ability to
analyze and assess. We imagine all kinds of scenarios. We write
the scripts of future encounters and rewrite those from the past:
"I could have said this and then they wouldn't have said that . . ."
and so on. However, the downside of this ability is that our

imagination can run away with itself. We can obsess, suffer from "analysis paralysis," and just not live "in the moment."

Our minds are often anywhere but in the moment—usually they prefer the past or the future. Meditation allows us to develop the ability to truly live in the moment—with practice, this makes us more effective in our ability to read the images and signs we see about our future or the future of our friends or clients.

What to do about those thoughts? The main thing is to expect that they will pop up in rapid succession the minute you decide to meditate. Acceptance is part of the cure. Once they begin, you can do a number of things to help slow and eventually quell them:

1 Imagine the thoughts attached to fluffy white clouds drifting across a perfect blue sky and see them float away.

2 See the thoughts as banners moving across your "mind screen"—like a computer screen saver—and then disappearing off the screen altogether.

3 Name the thoughts or categorize them, especially if they stay a little longer without drifting by easily. This can help diffuse them, because by naming them you limit their power to distract you. For example, you may categorize a confrontation you have remembered as "anger." If you remember that you are meant to call someone, tell yourself to recall this right after you cease meditating and then let the thought go, knowing that you will remember later—and you will.

4 Spend some time being the observer of your thoughts. Step onto the "observation platform" and watch the thoughts go by like waves or like trains. By simply observing them, as if you are an outsider, you don't feel the need to become involved with them. They simply come less frequently until finally you realize how still your mind has become.

It is best not to judge how you are "performing" the meditation. Do not become annoyed with yourself or judgmental if you have trouble stilling your mind. Some days you will slip into stillness the way you slip into a pair of favorite slippers. Other days you will feel as though you have to crawl through a minefield to reach some quiet in your mind.

Just accept that each meditative state will bring with it a different experience and enjoy the variety it brings.

AVOIDING ENERGY DRAINS

Use meditative techniques to help you deal with friends or clients who are going through a difficult period. Meditation helps shield you from your friend's or client's problems and fears. Difficult times are often the times when people feel a great desire to know what their future will bring. They are usually in need of comfort and want reassurance that they will get through their current issues.

Some believe that we have a core of pure energy that radiates outward through our physical body and beyond, surrounding our body with an aura of energy. The human aura is indeed an energy field. We are all connected and come from the same universal energy, which is why when we are in a meditative state we are able to tap into another person's life and to "read" their future.

On the negative side, this is also why another person's imbalance can drain us, if we are not careful to avoid this. For example, you may be doing a reading for a person who tends to overdramatize, who sees every event as a crisis. These people usually revel in their behavior and enjoy gaining attention—a form of energy—from other people's reactions and behaviors during their "performances." You will notice that you will feel drained when you are around them.

To avoid being inadvertently drained of your own energy during a fortune-telling session it is often best to observe the energy interplay with detached emotions, simply choosing not to become involved. This is one of the best ways to retain your energy. If you have been asked to do a reading for a person who you find depletes your energy, do your relaxation meditation (see pages 18–19) and white lighting exercise (see pages 20–21) and then focus again on breathing slowly and deeply.

Now picture yourself on the top of a hill, standing under a tree, overlooking a valley and other hills. Notice all the different shades of green in the grass and trees, and how blue the sky is. There are soft clouds drifting overhead and the sun is caressing your skin warmly. A gentle breeze is blowing and you notice the trees are swaying slightly.

Look at the energy pouring out of the trees and grass and picture it swirling around your body. Feel the energy pouring out of the tree you are standing beneath and look up into its magnificent branches. Stand with your back against the tree and feel its energy softly surround your body. As you stand quietly, you will notice that

you cannot feel where your body ends and where the tree and air begin. You softly melt into the tree and become one with it. You can feel the energy course through your body, with the strength of the tree becoming your own. The wisdom of the ages found in this ancient tree pours into your being.

Stand there, allowing the energies of the tree to pour through you, bringing inner strength and compassion for all living things. Become immersed in endless time and nothingness for as long as you like.

Now slowly begin to feel the boundaries of your body and see yourself stepping out of the tree trunk. Picture your energy combining with that of the tree and imagine the beautiful flow of energy between you.

Slowly bring yourself back to your room, bringing with you feelings of peace and contentment. Wiggle your fingers and toes and become aware once more of your breathing.

KEEPING YOUR SENSE OF OBJECTIVITY

One skill that is essential when giving fortune-telling readings is remaining objective, even when your friend or client is feeling overly stressed or unbalanced. What is objectivity? It is the ability to relate to others without becoming affected by personal bias or emotions. This does not mean that you have to be cold and indifferent. To be objective is to be able to step out of the picture and be detached emotionally, so that you can "respond" to the other person rather than "react."

We all have "buttons" that, when pressed by the comments or demands of others, elicit in us what is called a knee-jerk reaction. This is usually an uncomfortable reaction that brings with it feelings of inferiority, inadequacy, anger, fear, or anxiety. All of these feelings throw us off-center and disturb our ability to feel peaceful. Fear is usually at the bottom of these reactions: fear of ridicule, of being used, of being inadequate, and of giving too much. They all feel like valid fears, but if you allow inharmonious relations to develop because of fear, you will only exacerbate the fears and their harmful effect.

To achieve objectivity you need to maintain a centered state and become more of an observer than a participant in these situations. To observe involves looking at all the people involved in the interaction with detachment. For example, step into the other person's shoes to see what fears or emotions cause him to act the way he does. When a person is behaving aggressively toward you, ask yourself what he is fearful of, or what is going on in his life that makes him act that way.

Try to avoid feeling indignant or reacting without thinking. Thinking about and deciding on your response before you make it, which is what you need to do in these situations, is a liberating experience. It frees you from having to be involved emotionally and from allowing the situation to drain your energy. Consider how you would like to respond, and decide whether or not you really need to respond at all.

To help you develop this skill in your life, use the exercise below on a regular basis. Use scenarios you have already experienced as examples. If you do become involved in an upsetting conversation with someone, as is possible from time to time, use this exercise to see how it could have been avoided. Then try to use what you learn next time you need such objectivity—but during the actual conversation rather than afterward, on reflection.

OBJECTIVITY EXERCISE

Sit quietly and focus on breathing deeply and slowly for several minutes. Think of a time when you were relating with someone in a way that caused emotional discomfort. Replay the "movie" of this interaction in detail, reliving all the emotions you experienced at the time.

Imagine yourself stepping onto an "observer's platform" and watch the movie again—without judgment, and with compassion for both the people on the screen. Look closely at the person who is interacting with you and consider where her fears lie, why she was speaking to you in that way and why she reacted the way she did. Then look closely at your role: What were your fears? What made you react the way you did?

Replay the entire scene, this time using dialogue and behavior that are full of compassion and love, that come from a state of objectivity and detachment. See how the other person would then respond, rather than react, to your considered words and how you would have had a more harmonious interaction. And then look at yourself and consider the underlying causes of your reactions.

Unlocking Your Intuition

WHAT IS INTUITION?

Every person is born with the basis of that inner sense we call "intuition." Intuition is our innate warning system. If we allow it to, it will warn us of trouble or danger and will help us make decisions. Basic intuition, once trusted, can be developed into ESP (extrasensory perception) or psychic ability.

Intuition begins with instinct. Instinct is a universal gift from nature to all living things; it is a unity of the five senses—seeing, hearing, feeling, tasting, and smelling—that is unimpaired by either time or space. Instinct enables organisms to live, procreate, and survive. Hippocrates, the fifth century B.C. Greek philosopher known as the father of medicine, wrote: "[Intuition] is the instinct of the earlier races, when cold reason had not as yet obscured man's inner vision. . . . Its indication must never be disdained, for it is to instinct alone that we owe our first remedies."

Intuition is knowing that something is so, even in the absence of objective evidence. Intuition immediately reaches into the heart of the matter; it enables you to grasp art, music, and beauty and is at the base of humankind's desire for knowledge.

Insight is intuiting some truth, being able to make sense of that truth and express that understanding to others. Insight brings a

---

SOME FACTS ABOUT INTUITION

* Intuition is receiving energy in the form of feelings or "vibes" that make you "know" something significant about the person, event, or place associated with it.
* You must never use your mind, your intellect, or your sense of reason to analyze your "message," no matter how incongruous or strange it is. If you do, you will contaminate the experience with what you think you know—your intuition, on its own, will pick up on variables of which you are consciously unaware and which can have significant effects on a person, situation, or place.
* You cannot force intuition to happen—you can only open yourself to receive it.

person peace and a certainty that he or she can perceive the truth. People known for their insight do not allow material arguments (logic) to deter them; they are confident in their knowledge, whether or not it is reinforced by evidence.

ESP is intuition and insight developed to a very high level. It is the awareness of an event or influence without help from material evidence. When a person can intuit an external object, event, or influence, he or she is known as clairvoyant. Intuiting the mind of another person is known as telepathy. When a person can "see" into the future, it is called precognition.

It is sometimes most difficult to tell the difference between our intuition and our hopes and fears when we have an emotional investment in the situation or great expectations from it. This is because when we are emotionally involved we tend to stack the evidence in our own favor—this is normal and natural; however, it is not a good position to be in when trying to determine the truth of the matter.

When your intuition is at work, you are conscious of receiving some information that you know to be true. There is a sense of peace or quiet about this knowledge. You can look at it as something that originated outside yourself. This may cause you distress or great joy, but that sense of quiet is behind whatever other emotions you may experience as a result of the message— in fact, your response would be similar if you learned something important, and which you knew to be true, from another person.

DEVELOPING YOUR INTUITION

If you really wish to know the truth about something—something where you have a great deal to lose or gain—breathe in and out, gradually slowing your breathing until you are in a state of mental relaxation. While breathing, starting from the top of your head, focus on relaxing each part of your body. Once you are in a state of calm, mentally step back and view the situation as though it were happening to someone else. Whatever you pick up in this state will likely be truth, knowledge gained from your intuition.

The following exercise is a good one to help you develop your intuition because it helps you practice not having an emotional investment in any of the feelings you may pick up.

Choose a sunny day, one that is not too hot or too cold, and go sit in a park. Choose a time of day when some people will be sitting on the grass, in groups or by themselves, and others are walking by. Practice a meditation exercise, such as the one on pages 18–19, or breathe slowly, deeply, and evenly until you are feeling loose,· physically and mentally. You should now be conscious of bird sounds, traffic, people's voices—but feel detached from them all.

Now, allow yourself to be aware of the people around you and those who are wandering by. Remember, you can't order intuitive messages to come to you, you just need to be open to receive them. While you may pick up many faint intuitive messages, there will probably be at least one that you would like to focus on, strengthening your connection with it.

You may receive these messages as feelings or as factual knowledge. You may receive them in your solar plexus or through your "third eye," in the center of your forehead. The physical feeling you get from your intuition is very personal, but it could feel like a sense of excitement, anticipation, or unease.

Many intuitive messages can be quite abstract, so if you pick up something, quietly and calmly ask yourself some questions:

- What does the experience feel like? Good? Bad? Happy? Sad? Excited? Bitter?
- Has it affected my mood? For instance, do I feel a sudden depression or joy that was not mine to begin with?
- Does it leave almost as quickly as it came—for instance, once the person has passed by? Or does it linger? If so, for how long?

While you are sitting in the park, you will no doubt encounter a few passersby who will engage you in casual conversation. You will very likely enjoy these encounters; however, if you should suddenly feel uneasy, afraid, chilled, or nauseous for no apparent reason, despite the friendly overtures being made by the other person, you could safely assume that your intuition has kicked in.

It will help to make a list of key words that best describe the impressions you receive during this exercise, such as "natural," "unusual," "uneasy," "exciting," "frightening," "sad," and "joyful." Identify and note your feelings—preferably in a journal—shortly after the experience. Then, under the headings "who," "what," "where," "when," "how," and "why," identify and explain to yourself the entire experience, keeping in mind that you are dealing with your reactions to the experience.

COMMUNICATING WITH YOUR GUARDIAN ANGEL

Using your intuition to communicate with your guardian angel (see also pages 84–91) is easy if you exercise your intuitive powers regularly. Form a habit of meditating for half an hour each day in a suitable atmosphere, such as your favorite room; light six white candles to represent your six senses (intuition is your sixth sense); play some relaxing music, and think of all the things your intuition tried to tell you to do during the day. Note whether you actually listened to your intuition or whether you were simply reacting to your fears.

Using Creative Visualization

Creative visualization is sometimes called "active meditation" or "seeing with the mind's eye." Many familiar forms of Eastern meditation involve eliminating imagery from consciousness altogether, thereby removing the distractions provided by the chatter of the mind.

However, although creative visualization can be regarded as a form of meditation, it has a somewhat different emphasis. Rather than negating visual imagery, it involves summoning into our sphere of perception specific images that are helpful in providing insights and solutions to personal issues in our life. This technique can be successfully used in conjunction with virtually all fortune-telling techniques.

Some people claim that they are not especially gifted visually, that they don't see pictorial images when they close their eyes and enter the inner world we associate with the imagination. However, unless we were born blind, each one of us has the potential to create visual images, even if we are out of practice and have lost the knack for doing so. One way to start doing this is by focusing on each of the senses in turn.

Let's begin by identifying the following—sight, smell, touch, taste, hearing, and movement. Sit in a comfortable position, close your eyes, and relax. Now switch your attention completely to seeing—focusing all your powers of inner awareness on one of the following items:

- a golden sun
- a silver crescent moon
- a blue circle
- a red triangle
- a colorful bird flying through the air

Did you notice any bodily sensation as you focused on these images? Did these specific visual images provoke any associated sensations? What color was the bird? What type of bird was it?

Now try concentrating on smell. Begin by imagining the smells that appeal to you as well as those that repel you, bringing them all as fully as you can into your conscious awareness. For example, focus on the delicious smell of freshly baked bread or a freshly peeled orange or any other aroma you find enticing. Now try to recall the decidedly unpleasant smell of a carton of sour milk

that you have discovered in the back of your refrigerator.

Next, concentrate on your sense of touch. Imagine in your mind's eye that you are running your fingers across someone else's skin. Feel the softness and perhaps also the wrinkles, the little bumps and grooves, the textures that make the surface of the skin so distinctive. Now imagine stroking your hand through soft snow, or under running water, or across smooth, warm sand. What impressions come to mind as you do this? Do any particular associations emerge from your store of personal memories?

Now focus your awareness on your sense of taste. Recall that delicious cup of tea or coffee, or that scrumptious muffin that you had at breakfast, or the distinctive taste of a particular type of fruit juice or alcoholic beverage that you really enjoyed recently. Feel the taste on your lips.

Turn your attention to your sense of hearing. Listen to the distinctive song of a bird outside in the garden, or concentrate on the qualities of a particular person's voice. Recall the distinctive sound of bells chiming in a church or cathedral. What is it that makes these sounds so distinctive? Do any of these sounds evoke a particular emotional resonance for you? Are any of them associated with a particular memory?

Finally, focus your conscious awareness on your sense of movement. In your mind's eye, imagine first that you are walking, then running, and finally dancing. Now visualize swimming in a pool, or driving a car. Feel that sense of movement as you visualize these activities. Imagine how it feels to really be there.

As we gradually become attuned to our senses, images and sensory impressions will become stronger and clearer, enhancing our ability to see into the future.

USING CREATIVE VISUALIZATION TO CONTACT YOUR SPIRIT GUIDES

Many people like to practice a form of visualization that involves contacting their inner guides. You may regard your inner guides as personifications of your inner self or higher spiritual potential, or you may think of them as external beings—like angels or spirits (see pages 84–91)—who intercede on your behalf to heighten your powers of intuition or bring you wisdom and inspiration.

They can be male or female or figures from the ancient or mythical past. They can be familiar or eccentric and unconventional. The important thing is to trust that your inner guide can bring to your realm of conscious awareness insights and information that you will find useful in your everyday life, information that probably would not have become available to you through more familiar and conventional processes.

However we think of them, inner guides exist in a realm beyond our direct conscious awareness. We can, however, use our powers of creative visualization to make contact with them. Here is a creative visualization exercise for contacting your inner guide.

- Close your eyes and enter a state of deep relaxation using the techniques described earlier in this book. Now visualize that you are journeying on a path toward a special, sacred place. It is a place that is safe and secret—a place known only to you.

- Now, as you venture further along this path, notice a figure in the distance coming toward you. The figure shines with radiant light, emanating a feeling of tranquility and deep knowing—you realize that this is your inner guide. As your guide comes closer, you are able to tell whether this figure is male or female. You also take note of the garments this person is wearing, whether the being is young or old, and other distinctive aspects of his or her external appearance.

- Greet your guide, ask for his or her name, and then proceed together to your special sacred place. When you arrive, show your guide around, explain why this place is sacred to you, and make him or her feel welcome. Then ask your guide some specific questions or inquire whether there is something he or she wishes to impart to you. Some answers may be forthcoming immediately; if not, don't panic. Your questions will be answered later.

- When the meeting with your guide seems to have reached some form of conclusion, thank this figure of light, ask him or her to make contact with you again in the future, and make your way back down the path to your familiar everyday world. When you feel ready, open your eyes.

Your inner guide is a special being whom you may call on whenever you are in need of special insights, intuition, wisdom, or loving advice. You may wish to keep a diary to write down the insights or intuitions you receive from your inner guide, and to keep a record of how you have applied these lessons in your everyday life.

You may call upon your spirit guide before giving a psychic reading. Your spirit guide can help you tap into the issues that face your client or friend and help you see more clearly into the future.

ENHANCING YOUR PSYCHIC ABILITY

Developing Your Psychic Ability

TESTING THE TAROT: FOCUSING ON A SINGLE CARD
The exercises in this chapter can be practiced on your own or
with a friend if another person is needed. Psychic circles use these
exercises, or ones like them, at every meeting.

The tarot cards provide students of psychic phenomena with
ample opportunity for psychic development—in particular the
twenty-two cards of the Major Arcana. Each card in the Major
Arcana has a descriptive title and is full of symbols, all of which
have specific meanings. The reader is supposed to study these
symbols to further enrich his or her interpretation of the card (see
pages 166–177).

A common exercise is to choose one of the Major Arcana
tarot cards, examine it closely, and write down your immediate
impressions of the card. Once you have recorded your first
impression, look at the card again, for a longer period of time, to
interpret the meanings of the card. It is believed that each card
takes on another meaning if the card is "reversed," or turned upside
down. Reverse your chosen Major Arcana card and go through
he same procedure. This is an excellent exercise to inspire you to
test your intuitive skills by extracting every possible piece of
information from the card.

As an example, let us assume that you have been interpreting
card No. VII, entitled "The Chariot." The picture reveals an armored
soldier steering his chariot. Two horses draw the chariot, one white
and one black. Everything about the picture suggests that the
soldier has perfect control of the vehicle and the horses. In the
background we see a picture that suggests affluence—tall, stately
buildings and lush green fields. The chariot is ornate, and curtains
decorated by glistening stars adorn it. The soldier wears a crown
whose centerpiece is a star.

The card holds both a spiritual and material meaning.
On the spiritual level: If you are looking for the spiritual

enlightenment this card offers, you will see that the message this picture is giving you is that you are the person responsible for the spiritual safety of your vehicle (the soul or conscience). You have been given every advantage to aid you in your safety (represented by the armor and a good pair of horses). The affluence depicted suggests that your spiritual guidance is positive. Everything is in your favor for a safe and straight journey through life.

The black and white horses represent the positive and negative forces you must deal with on your journey. If you examine the soldier's face, you will see that he is focused on the road ahead. This is the example you must follow if you wish to avoid accidents and setbacks. When this card is in the upright position, it represents the fact that you are taking control of your spiritual life in a safe and orderly fashion.

Reversed, it means that you are temporarily out of control. You are traveling in a spiritually damaged vehicle and allowing temporary distractions to cause you harm.

On the material level: The chariot represents the vehicle you drive, such as a bicycle or car. The vehicle is mechanically safe and is capable of being driven in good and bad conditions (the black and white horses). When this card appears in your layout, it suggests that you are about to take a journey that is assured of safety and comfort.

Reversed, it represents mechanical faults in the vehicle that will cause accidents. This card also appears in the reversed position when the driver (you) is proceeding in a careless manner or is under the

influence of alcohol or drugs. Either way, it always predicts accidents, but not fatalities.

Summary: All this information, spiritual or material, is contained in this one card. When you review it, you will see that by concentrating on the picture and extending your intuition, it all makes perfect sense. The results of this exercise should encourage you to take the time and effort to develop your psychic abilities.

TELEPATHY

Telepathy is a direct mental communication between two people: a transmitter and a receiver. A transmitter will use pictures, signs, words, or sentences, which she or he can send to a receiver who is able to identify what was sent.

Geographical distance will not interfere with the transmission of telepathic messages. While laboratory tests aimed at proving the power of telepathy have been inconclusive, they seem able to identify who is the receiver and who is the transmitter. As is the case with most other methods of psychic communication, real-life experiences offer the more profound evidence.

As an example, take the case of two cousins, at the time aged thirteen and eleven years old, who enjoyed playing a game they called "Guess What?" As they explained it to their parents, one girl would conjure up a picture in her mind of some object, person, or scene, which she then "sent" to her cousin's mind. Her cousin would then interpret the message she was receiving. She was seldom wrong.

As years have passed, the girls have periodically tested themselves to see if they are still able to transmit and receive messages from each other using this method of communication, and indeed they can. The only time they fail the test is when they try to reverse their roles of transmitter and receiver. This suggests that one girl can only transmit messages and the other can only receive them.

In some psychic workshops, similar tests are used. For instance, a partition (usually a screen) is placed between two of the students. One is given a pack of the Major Arcana cards from the tarot. These cards are often used because their colors and detail are well defined. The student shuffles the pack, cuts it into two, places both stacks face up, and then concentrates on the pictures.

WARNING

Never try to transmit a negative thought to another person or suggest that they do something that you know that they wouldn't or shouldn't do. Similarly, no one can make you do something you don't want to do.

Two cards are now showing, and the receiver is asked to describe them. The more detail he can give about the card, the higher his telepathic power is rated. The students always find this part of their psychic development entertaining as well as useful. It is also fascinating to discover who are the transmitters and who are the receivers. Those who are psychically well developed seem to be able to play either role.

Another fun exercise to try with a friend is called "What Were You Doing on Sunday?" For seven consecutive Sundays, one of you should choose an activity such as drawing, writing, or reading, which you would think of or act out at the specified time (say 10:00 A.M.). Try to transmit the idea to your friend. Prearrange that at 10:15 A.M. she will call and tell you what she thought you were doing at 10:00 A.M.

In another exercise, prearrange with your friend that you will take an object belonging to her, such as a comb or a book, and hide it. Now try to visualize and transmit the hiding place to her. See if she can go to the right spot and find the hidden object. See how many times out of three, five, or seven your friend finds the object. Then change places and see if you can receive the information.

If you are finding these exercises fairly easy, you have natural psychic ability. If you are having some difficulties, don't worry— just continue practicing regularly. You will improve with time. It is important not to feel tense about getting it "right." You will do your best work when you are feeling relaxed (see the relaxation meditation on pages 18–19).

Going to Psychic Workshops

Reputable psychic workshops, which teach you all the various methods of fortune-telling from an elementary to an advanced level, are not easy to locate. But, like any school of learning, it is worth the effort you put into finding the best to become the best.

The only prerequisites you need to join a psychic workshop are a mind free of restraints and a desire to contribute as much positive psychic energy as you desire to receive. These workshops are a team effort.

Collective psychic energy creates great power, and much good can come out of the meditative influences in a psychic circle. The intention of workshops is for the students and teachers to combine their efforts and energies in the development of mutual psychic awareness.

Meditation, psychometry, palmistry, numerology, card reading, and tea-leaf and coffee grounds reading are a few of the fortune-telling skills you will learn to master. Creating the right atmosphere with music, color, chanting, and the burning of powerful but discreet aromatic essences and candles during a meditation period will enhance individual and collective spiritual and psychic growth.

Psychic workshops have the same advantages and disadvantages as any other group. You may not always have a completely compatible set of colleagues or teachers. However, as life is a continual challenge, we must strive to improve conditions and to overcome our limitations.

Throughout the world, regardless of creed or culture, people continue to seek answers to their personal problems and to look for solutions to life's adversities. Psychic workshops do not have all the answers, but they do teach you how to develop the skills that will help you find answers to these often life-altering questions.

The innately curious nature of human beings creates an insatiable appetite for the skills of fortune-telling, hence the popularity of psychic workshops. Although these centers attract genuine students, they can also attract emotionally insecure people, who become dependent on fortune-telling to solve all their problems. This is not how fortune-telling is meant to be used. These people often forget to use logic and common sense to run their day-to-day lives. This can then lead to a most unhealthy version of self-obsession. It is important to remember that you are responsible for the choices you make in life; you are not a victim.

There are also periods of time when, for your own sake, as well as the sake of your peers, it is wise to take a break from a workshop. Negative forces affect everyone at some time or another. If you are experiencing serious nervous disorders, illness, or emotional upheaval, for instance, you are likely going through a time of self-pity and self-indulgence, and this is detrimental to teamwork.

It may be better to become involved with some alternative recreation, such as athletic activities and entertainment, during these times. This way you will gradually rebuild your psychic energy and can return to your psychic workshop activities with a new and positive attitude.

It is not uncommon to find that some students miss classes or change workshops frequently. This has a negative effect on everyone. Consistency is an important ingredient in developing psychic ability, so unless you are experiencing difficulty because of incompatibility with your workshop peers, you should strive to be persistent and consistent.

The importance of student compatibility

Compatibility between the students and their teachers can make the difference between rapid and slow psychic development for the whole group. A good teacher will have discreetly engineered a situation where he or she is able to examine your interaction with the other students.

Sometimes, however, a purely self-serving student will slip through, and it takes only one person's insincerity to disrupt the flow of the good psychic energy that a compatible psychic group can generate.

Trust

Many guarded family secrets are inadvertently brought to light during psychic meetings with guardian angels and the spirits of deceased relatives. In one particularly sensitive example a young woman tried to contact the spirit of her deceased father, who supposedly died when she was three years old, and who was apparently born and raised in England. This young woman was raised in an orphanage with antiquated rules, so her family history was sketchy.

The psychic workshop group was surprised to learn from the spirit of a deceased American that he was her father. It seems she was the result of an adulterous affair between himself and her mother, also deceased. He went on to explain that he had wanted to raise his daughter but was encouraged to leave the country. As a result of this she was left with her mother and stepfather, who both abandoned her. He told her that the man she called "Father" was still alive and living in England. It was a traumatic but enlightening story—which, by the way, all proved to be true.

This kind of shared information builds a trustful bond among members of the group. It is very important to keep confidential information about others in your group to yourself.

Negative thinkers

It is not uncommon for people experiencing an emotionally disturbed period in their lives to become negative in their thoughts, words, and deeds. When this kind of energy is brought into a psychic workshop situation it is a natural deterrent to good psychic power; it can even attract unwelcome spirits into the workshop space. Like attracts like, and just as the person in emotional trauma becomes dependent on the positive energy of the other members of the group, so too do the disturbed spirits the person attracts.

This is not to say that everyone should desert a fellow member who is suffering. On the contrary, you are in a powerful position to help this person reverse their negative period if he or she is prepared to listen and trust you to act in his or her best interests. If this help is refused, encourage your troubled friend to take time out from psychic development until he or she is able to prioritize.

As for the unwelcome spirit visitors—they are much more difficult to persuade to leave. You could try the circle of white light and some affirmations or other psychic shields to combat the negativity they create (see pages 54–61).

When your psychic ability is well developed, you can also detect a negative person's vibration in everyday life. Under these conditions, if you cannot avoid the person, the fastest and easiest method is to visualize the circle of white light being placed around you so that the negative energy emitted by his or her aura cannot penetrate your own aura (see also the various meditation techniques on pages 20–21 and 24–25).

Choosing Your Fortune-Telling Technique

After you have worked with various fortune-telling techniques for a while and have developed your psychic abilities, you will start to favor one method of psychic craft over all the others you have learned, much like a person who gets a business degree and then goes on to be an accountant, or someone who studies medicine and goes on to specialize in pediatrics.

Palmistry is a craft that offers an interesting challenge. If you feel that palmistry may become your specialty, remember that there are just as many complexities to learn here as there are in any other psychic discipline.

Once you understand the idea that palmistry is a map etched out in the palms of your hands, and compare the Main Lines—the Life Line, the Heart Line, the Head Line—with the main highways of your journey through life, and the Minor Lines (Marriage, Children, Health, and Travel) to the other roadways on your journey, then the study of palmistry becomes infinitely interesting and appealing.

Learning palmistry, like any other psychic discipline—divination through cards, numbers, stones, coins, crystals, or the stars—is not an easy task. If you decide to specialize in any of these crafts, you must apply yourself from the beginning with dedication.

There is a belief that certain types of people resonate with a particular fortune-telling skill. In many Western magical traditions there is a belief that people can be categorized as being predominantly one of the four elements—earth, air, fire, and water. In astrology, one way of determining what kind of element you are is to see whether you were born under a certain sun sign.

See if one of the following descriptions seems to apply to your character. Remember that sometimes people have more than one dominant element affecting their personality. Check some of the other descriptions and see if you would like to investigate other types of divination.

Earth

An earth type of person is practical and "down to earth"; if desiring to enhance her psychic abilities, she would be more interested in using divination tools such as stones (see pages

162–165) and runes (see pages 148–151). In Western astrology, earth elements include those who were born under the sun signs of Taurus, Virgo, and Capricorn (see pages 62–63).

Air

An air type of person is academic and likes complex theories and abstract concepts. They usually feel comfortable with such divination tools as astrology (see pages 62–71), *I Ching* (see pages 92–97), numerology (see pages 98–117), certain forms of scrivening (see pages 152–155), and the tarot (see pages 166–177). In Western astrology, air elements include those who were born under the sun signs of Gemini, Libra, and Sagittarius (see pages 62–63).

Fire

A fire type of person is quick-witted, impulsive, and is capable of short bursts of strong psychic energy. This type of person would

enjoy aura readings (see page 72), dice (see pages 82–83), spells (see pages 156–161), and wax reading (see pages 182–183). In Western astrology, fire elements include those who were born under the sun signs of Aries, Leo, and Sagittarius (see pages 62–63).

Water

A water type of person is able to tap into their own emotions as well as the issues of their friends and clients. They are sensitive and would particularly enjoy palmistry (see pages 118–143), certain forms of scrivening (see pages 152–155), tea-leaf or coffee grounds reading (see pages 178–181), and wax reading (see pages 182–183). In Western astrology, water elements include those who were born under the sun signs of Cancer, Scorpio, and Pisces (see pages 62–63).

A Moon Talisman and Other Objects

TALISMANS AND AMULETS

Talismans and amulets come in all shapes and sizes. Two talismans used for protection in psychic circles are drawings or figurines of the lotus and the moon. The moon is a powerful symbol of intuition and magic, and helps you unlock your intuitive potential.

There is a powerful celestial talisman you can make that resonates with the energy of the moon. To make a moon talisman, you will need a silver-colored disk of either metal or cardboard, a black permanent marker, and a silver-colored drawstring bag. On a Monday, draw on one side of your disk the following symbol:

On the other side of the disk, draw the following box and numbers:

37	78	29	70	21	62	13	54	5
6	38	79	30	71	22	63	14	46
47	7	39	80	31	72	23	55	15
16	48	8	40	81	32	64	24	56
57	17	49	9	41	73	33	65	25
26	58	18	50	1	42	74	34	66
67	27	59	10	51	2	43	75	35
36	68	19	60	11	52	3	44	76
77	28	69	20	61	12	53	4	45

Keep this simple talisman safe in the drawstring bag and carry it in a left-hand pocket—the left side is symbolic of your intuitive side.

FORTUNE-TELLER'S TIP

Certain crystals have the energy to repel evil influences; they can be carried on your person, placed in appropriate positions, or put under your pillow. Coral beads are reputed to ward off bad luck. The crucifix is one of many religious talismans worn for spiritual inspiration and protection from evil. An iron horseshoe is not only reputed to attract good luck but also believed to stop the devil or an evil energy entering your home or psychic space, particularly if the horseshoe is hung over your door with its ends pointing up.

CHOOSING OTHER OBJECTS TO ENHANCE YOUR SKILLS

Over the centuries, certain stones and herbs that help enhance a person's intuitive and psychic abilities have been identified. Simply by carrying these stones or herbs, either singly or in a certain combination, you'll find that you will easily be able to tap into your intuitive side. This will help you improve your fortune-telling skills.

When you are setting up your special psychic space (see pages 52–61) you may wish to decorate the room with one of the following flowers or keep some of the following herbs (see table below) in a bowl near you. You may also wish to burn one of the essential oils in the table below while you are giving a fortune-telling reading.

Some fortune-tellers like to store their magical tools, such as their tarot cards, runes, or stones, with some flowers, herbs, or a couple of drops of essential oil on a cloth that can be wrapped around the cards or other items to keep them safe from negative energy.

There are also some excellent stones that you can wear around your neck or carry in your left pocket to help enhance your fortune-telling skills. These include:

- clear crystal
- moonstone
- mother of pearl
- pearl
- sapphire

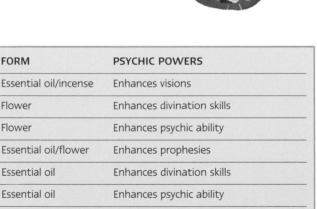

PLANT	FORM	PSYCHIC POWERS
Cedar	Essential oil/incense	Enhances visions
Hibiscus	Flower	Enhances divination skills
Honeysuckle	Flower	Enhances psychic ability
Jasmine	Essential oil/flower	Enhances prophesies
Orange	Essential oil	Enhances divination skills
Peppermint	Essential oil	Enhances psychic ability
Rose	Essential oil/flower	Enhances divination skills (particularly with respect to questions about love)
Saffron	Herb	Enhances psychic ability
Sandalwood	Essential oil/incense	Enhances visions
Thyme	Herb	Enhances psychic ability

Working During a Full Moon

A full moon is one of the most powerful psychic times of the moon's cycle. Traditionally, it was thought that the fullness of the moon related to a raised level of psychic energy, which could be harnessed for a number of magical purposes as well as fortune-telling.

You may notice that if you do a reading during the full moon, your insights and visions are more detailed and you cover many more issues. Readings given during the waning moon may seem to focus more on the endings of things, such as relationships or careers; readings given during a new moon will focus on new love, adventures, and prospects.

After some time you will notice that new moon readings tend to be more positive and deal more with the future, while waning moon readings tend to deal with problems and issues of the past. Sometimes when a friend or client asks you for a reading during a particular time of the moon's cycle, he or she is instinctively seeking answers to issues that are best resolved at those times.

Do not be disappointed if you are not able to see beyond a person's past problems in a reading—they may well need to deal with these issues before they can follow their true future path. However, if you feel that you may have blockages in your psychic energy, try cleansing your aura (see pages 50–51) so that you are able to "see" your visions more clearly or tap into your intuition more cleanly. Also, you may need to protect your energy if you are feeling drained (see pages 20–21 and 24–25).

Try the following full moon ritual to help you tap into the energy of the full moon for your fortune-telling reading or to

---

FORTUNE-TELLER'S TIP

There is a superstition that if you find a four-leaf clover on St. John's Eve you will gain supernatural powers. St. John's Eve is on June 23.

enhance your psychic development. On the night of the full moon, gather a white candle (and a match or lighter), some white flowers, a silver bowl filled with water, and a stone that resonates with the moon, such as a clear quartz crystal, an unset moonstone (preferably a round cabochon), or a disk of mother of pearl, plus your favorite divination tools and a piece of white cloth—make sure the cloth is big enough to wrap the tools completely in its folds.

If you can, place the candle in a stable holder and put it in the window from which you can see the moon. Place the silver bowl filled with fresh, clean water on a table or bookcase under the window so that, if at all possible, the moon's image is reflected in the water.

If you use a particular set of divination tools, such as a favorite tarot deck or a bag or runes, place them between the bowl of water and the window, so that moonlight shines upon your tools, cleansing them of any negative associations and enhancing their connection with the moon's heightened psychic influence.

Place them on the piece of white cloth. Do not wrap the tools in the white cloth yet, but position the moonstone, crystal, or mother of pearl on top of the tools.

Scatter the petals of the white flowers on the surface of the water in the silver bowl and light the candle. Say the following words:

Gentle face of our dear Mother Moon,
Before you lie my tools of divination,
Cleanse and enhance their psychic power,
So that they may be used in truth and wisdom,
Thank you, dear Mother Moon.

Blow out the candle and let the objects stay in place overnight. In the morning, wrap your divination tools in the white cloth with the stone or a moon talisman that you had made earlier (see page 46). If you are doing readings constantly, consider doing this simple ritual once every full moon.

Cleansing Your Aura

What is your aura? It is a form of energy generated by the vibrations in your body. To see your aura, sit or stand in front of a mirror with a dark or white background behind you. Half close your eyes and "look" at the energy field around your head. Can you make out a haze of rainbowlike colors around your head? This is your aura.

Try to determine whether the haze is close to your head or flaring out. When you are nervous, the aura around your head (a nimbus) is often close to your head or quite dark. If you have psychic or physical blocks in your body, the aura will be close to your body or the colors may be muted or dull. Your aura can also be temporarily damaged by negative energy in the atmosphere around you.

The aura needs to be cleansed so that you are able to resist negative attitudes and psychic leeches. This is particularly important when you are giving fortune-telling readings or if you are trying to strengthen your psychic abilities.

Try this simple aura-cleansing exercise before you give a fortune-telling reading. You will need a full-length mirror, a small table onto which you place a white candle, something to light the candle with, an essential oil burner, some lemongrass essential oil, a small dish of water, and a card or paper containing the following aura-cleansing affirmation:

This is my aura, it belongs to me,
It is a vital part of my being.
I evoke my intuitive power to
Open my mind and my eyes to the
Beauty of the color and the light within.

Begin burning the lemongrass oil and light the candle. Stand in front of the mirror, about one foot away from it. Take a deep breath, inhaling deeply, and then hold your breath for a few seconds; exhale slowly. Repeat five times.

Now look into the mirror and focus your attention at a point somewhere in the middle of your chest. Do not stare. Become aware that in your peripheral vision you are seeing some color outlining your body. Do not shift your eyes to focus on the color, simply be aware that something is there. Keep your focus like this for as long as you feel comfortable—you may find that the color and shape of the aura are strengthening.

Now let your eyes drift to a point about six inches above your head. You may be able to see color or a hazy shape around your head. Do not stare, but keep your eyes almost half-closed. Let your eyes drift to a point about six inches to the sides of your arms, and then to a point the same distance from your legs.

As you continue to glance around the outside of your body in this semitrance state, try to meditate and visualize this energy field as you chant the words of your affirmation. Repeat the affirmation until you are feeling serene and fully present in your body.

Take some time to get acquainted with your aura. Try this exercise three days or evenings in a row. Do the exercise either at the beginning of the day, as close to dawn as possible, or in the evening, during the twilight period. These times are excellent for helping you see into new worlds.

Sometimes, the first time you are successful in seeing the aura, the excitement you feel may disturb the serenity of the atmosphere you have created and you may lose the picture. This is a natural occurrence, so don't be alarmed or disappointed. The next time you will be ready for it. With each attempt you are strengthening your chances of seeing your aura.

To close the cleansing ceremony, first sprinkle the water over your aura, then end by imagining that there is a cocoon of white light around you and your aura. This white light symbolizes an energy that will help protect you from harm and negativity.

A SAFE PSYCHIC ATMOSPHERE

Choosing a Suitable Psychic Space

Creating the right kind of positive energy is extremely important for your special place. The ambience needs to be calming and peaceful so that you can develop your psychic abilities and learn the art of fortune-telling.

Whatever environment you choose for your psychic and fortune-telling development, you should feel an intimacy with the vibration within its walls. While many people like the idea of conducting a psychic workshop outdoors, there are in fact too many distractions in nature that will disturb your proceedings—and which you would not want to interfere with anyway. When spiritual or religious ceremonies are conducted inside an enclosed space, the energy is contained within that area, increasing its power.

The place you choose should be well ventilated so that the psychic energy can easily flow to all parts of the room. Its size should be comfortable so that intimacy can be maintained. Remember that the place you choose will become your special psychic space, so it is important that it's a room that will not be entered by anyone other than you and whoever you invite to share the space for fortune-telling purposes. The space should also be as far from distracting noises as possible. If such a room is impossible to find in your home, maybe another member of your group has a suitable room in his or her house.

Before you start your psychic or fortune-telling activities, it is a good idea to begin to build up a psychic and joyous atmosphere. Start by carrying out a short meditation. Leave your divination tools in the space. Decorate the area with your favorite fabrics and objects. Images of stars and moons, as well as beads, lush fabrics, feathers, and lots of candles, should make this a special space for a retreat.

Before using the room for psychic work, cleanse the space (see pages 54–55), consider working within a psychic circle (see pages 56–59), and set up some protective shields (see pages 60–61).

CREATING A JOYOUS ATMOSPHERE

Whatever the occasion may be, it is only natural that we try to create an appropriate atmosphere. Weddings conjure up a joyous atmosphere that is enhanced by pretty flowers, satin, lace, and romantic music playing in the background. The guests adorn themselves with brightly colored clothing, and the atmosphere is alive with the aroma of many perfumes.

Creating a psychic environment deserves the same attention to detail as any other important event. Ambient music that includes the sounds of nature will relax and loosen the mind. Fabrics in psychic colors, such as soft blues, greens, and lilacs, can be draped around the area. The ethereal glow of white candles creates a psychic-enhancing atmosphere,  as does the aroma of essential oils such as lavender, which soothes the heart and mind.

For further psychic power, add crystals such as amethyst, which induces a state of tranquility; yellow fluorite, to help give a sense of inner peace while enhancing mental clarity; and tiger's eye, for balancing the emotions and awakening the intuition.

Positive energy encourages the development of your psychic awareness and evokes highly evolved spirits, who can more easily communicate under these conditions. Creating a joyous atmosphere for the space where you give fortune-telling readings and develop your psychic abilities puts the people for whom you are doing the readings on the same wavelength. This builds up a communicative energy, making it easier to give accurate readings and to have an enjoyable interaction.

If you work with a particular spirit or guardian angel, creating such a welcoming psychic space will make your spirit guide or guides feel welcome. They will help provide you with protection and assistance in connecting with the spirit world when you need to. To honor your guardian angel or other spirit guide, dedicate one section of your psychic space to them. Decorate this area with fresh flowers, scents, and statues and other objects that help you feel linked with this generous and helpful entity.

Cleansing the Space

B efore you move into the house that is to become your new
home, you clean the place thoroughly, then decorate it to suit
the needs and personality of you and your family. Similarly, you
need to cleanse the atmosphere in your new psychic space, to make
sure you have cleared out any old or negative energy that could
disturb the psychic power you wish to create.

The cleansing process is important, because positive psychic
energy attracts powerful spirit contact and promotes psychic
growth. You will find it easier to direct your thoughts to psychic
activities when there are no atmospheric distractions or
disturbances in your psychic space.

Another reason for cleansing the atmosphere before a psychic
session is to remove any unfriendly, unsuitable spirit visitors who
will otherwise be attracted to your space. They can be as difficult
to remove as a person who crashes a party. This is a time when
prevention is better than cure.

The first step is to thoroughly clean the space physically. Sweep
and dust the room, visualizing that you are sweeping away the
intangible negative psychic energy that has accumulated in spaces,
particularly where traumas or intense emotions, such as anger, have
been expressed.

Remove any clutter that has accumulated in the space. Clear the
room as completely as possible. Remember, if there is a lot of clutter
to deal with, the clearing will take some time—you will need to sort
through what has been accumulated and decide whether you want
to keep it or throw it out. If you are having problems removing the
clutter, hang a clear quartz crystal over it; you will soon notice that
you are finding ways to deal with the clutter bit by bit.

When you have cleaned the space and cleared it of any clutter,
ring a melodious-sounding bell in all the nooks and crannies of
the room. This will disrupt and disperse the final vestiges of
negative energy.

Now you will need to purify the space. Salt has been used as a
purifier for centuries, so sprinkle salt across each opening to the
room—doors, windows, and even air vents.

You may then wish to do the following ceremony to dedicate the
space to your psychic work. You will need a round table covered by
a white tablecloth onto which are placed the following objects: one

white candle, three drops each of three essential oils (lemongrass, frankincense, and myrrh), an oil burner, a tea light, some matches, a bowl of water, a small dish of table salt, a compass, and a piece of paper with the words of the following cleansing ceremony affirmation written on it:

> *I invoke the collective psychic forces of*
> *The universe to attend the cleansing of*
> *This establishment, and I dedicate this space to*
> *The purpose of true and wise psychic work.*

Place the table in the middle of your space, stand in front of it, light the candle, and say your affirmation. Measure out the essential oils into the oil burner and light the tea light. Ascertain where the four cardinal points of the compass lie in your space. Take the bowl to each cardinal point and sprinkle some water in that area. This represents a psychic cleansing of the space.

When you have done this, bring the bowl of water back to the table. Read out your affirmation again, then pick up the dish of table salt and sprinkle the salt around the edges of your psychic space in a circle, as a symbol of purification.

Return the dish to the table, and for the third and last time read out your affirmation. Take a moment to feel your newly cleansed space; enjoy the sensation. Extinguish the candle and tea light—the ceremony is now complete.

Creating a Psychic Circle

PREPARING FOR CASTING A PSYCHIC CIRCLE

A circle is thought to be a space between worlds, a space where it is possible to direct your psychic energy for the good of your soul and your community. The circle is a symbol of protection: it keeps you safe from unwanted negative energies and lets you concentrate your own positive energies within its confines.

You may wish to cast a psychic circle each time you engage in exercises that help you develop your psychic abilities or practice your fortune-telling techniques. You may also cast a psychic circle before each fortune-telling session for a client.

However, remember that as you are casting the circle from within the space, you will need to specially open the circle briefly to allow your client to come inside it. In this way both you and your client will be protected from negative influences. A client who is feeling particularly troubled by his or her issues will usually feel

some respite by simply sitting in your psychic circle.

Before casting your circle, you will need to have cleansed your space (see pages 54–55) and your body. Having a bath before you enter your special place to do any psychic work is a very effective way of clearing away all the troubles of the day. You will find that after doing such a cleansing, your psychic work will seem to be more effective—you will be able to focus more efficiently on your psychic work, and your mind will not be cluttered with everyday concerns.

All you need for a cleansing bath is a beeswax candle (and something to light it with), a large glass of cool, clean water, and some cedarwood or lavender essential oil. Measure out four drops of your chosen essential oil into the bath water. Set up the beeswax candle so that you can gaze at it while you are bathing. Light the candle and slip into the bath.

As you are soaking, take notice of all your senses. Check the taste in your mouth, taking a sip of water to cleanse your palate if

necessary. Notice the scent of the oils you have chosen. Create little waves in your tub with your hands; listen to the motion of the water and feel how it caresses your skin.

Allow your eyes to stare momentarily at the lighted candle. Close your eyes and imagine the candle flame in the middle of your forehead, your "third eye." Hold the image for as long as possible and then relax, with your eyes closed. This simple exercise will help you tap into your intuition.

Take the time to also visualize any stray thoughts of the day encapsulated in a bubble, floating away from you.

When you feel ready, get out of the bath, dry yourself with a fresh towel, and drain the tub, watching the water and all your worries go down the drain. You are now ready for your psychic work.

Put on fresh clothes; it is a good idea to have set aside clothing that you wear only for your psychic work. It is important that the clothes in which you do your psychic work are comfortable and fairly loose. Try to wear clothes that are made from natural fibers such as silk, cotton, linen, flax, wool, or even hemp, as these materials allow your skin to breathe.

If it is possible to make your own clothes, be generous with the quantity of fabric you use so that you can feel enfolded in fabric and can enjoy the sensation of the material on your skin.

CASTING AND CLOSING YOUR CIRCLE

Enter your psychic space after having purified it (see pages 54–55), and after you have cleansed and dressed yourself (see pages 56–57). Bring into the space the following ingredients, which you will need to cast your circle for a fortune-telling session: a white candle, a stable candleholder, a compass, your divination tools, sticks of frankincense and myrrh incense or your favorite incense, an incense holder, and matches.

Frankincense and myrrh are useful incenses for a psychic circle: frankincense both protects and cleanses magical spaces and aids a person's concentration, and myrrh will heighten your magical awareness. On a table or other stable surface in the room, set up the candle and the incense sticks.

Light them and sit in the middle of the room, either on the floor or in a comfortable chair, with your compass and your divination tools. Make sure that you are facing north in the northern hemisphere, south in the southern hemisphere. North is symbolic of the element of earth and represents your connection with the physical and psychic world.

Concentrate on your breathing. Breathe in for a count of four and then out for a count of four. Continue until you feel a sense of stillness and calm. You are now ready to cast your circle.

Stand up, holding your divination tools in your left hand (if you are using a number of tools, make a bag for them and hold that in your left hand). Stretch out your right hand and imagine that a glowing white energy is traveling from the earth up your legs and body, then down your arm to your fingertips. Walk in a circle around the room, as close to the walls as possible, in a clockwise direction, imagining that you are carving out a protective circle around you with the white energy as you cast your circle.

Once the circle is cast, place your divination tools on the table or surface that you will use for your fortune-telling session. At this point you may wish to invite a special spirit guide (see pages 34–35) or guardian angel (see pages 84–91) into your circle. Here is an example of how you may invite your guardian angel into a psychic circle:

In the name of this psychic circle, and in the
best interests of the development of psychic power,
we invoke the divine intervention of our guardian
angels to guide us in our psychic workshop activities.
We ask this in good faith and in the belief that our
achievement will benefit the universe.

When you feel ready, invite your friend or client for a fortune-telling session. You will need to cut open the circle to allow this person to enter your special space. You do not need to do this in front of him or her. All you have to do is again imagine the white light emanating from your fingertips, and make a motion of cutting the circle open in front of the door or other physical entrance into your psychic space. As your friend or client passes through the doorway, close the entrance by not only shutting the door but also by visualizing the white light sealing the doorway.

Once your fortune-telling session is over, visualize the doorway in the circle being opened, and allow your friend or client to walk out. Close your psychic circle as soon as possible after you have finished.

To close your circle, thank your spirit guide or guardian angel for attending and then walk counterclockwise around the room, imagining the white energy that defined your psychic circle being reeled back into your body and then flowing back into the ground under the floorboards. Your circle is now closed.

Setting Up Your Psychic Shields

Some people are so eager to develop their psychic ability that it never occurs to them that there are almost as many negative forces waiting to invade a psychic circle as there are positive ones, and so they leave themselves open to the dangers of entering the realms of the unknown without protection.

It is worth noting that while you may be very happy to contact the spirits of deceased loved ones, such power can also attract uninvited guests who may be harmless, but who don't want to leave. This is why casting a psychic circle (see pages 58–59) is so important.

Even if you don't have the time or space to cast a psychic circle, you can still protect yourself before doing a fortune-telling session at a friend's house or in a public area by visualizing a circle of white light around you and the area where you will be using your divination tools.

Imagine the white light as a brilliant halo, symbolizing purity and good intention, which will act as a protective shield. Once you have visualized this protective psychic cocoon around you, chant the words of the following affirmation:

May this pure circle of white light envelop me,
these objects and this environment,
so that no harm or ill intent may enter its vicinity.
I ask this protection for the sincere purpose
of the pursuit of psychic truth and wisdom.

Just as an explorer would not enter unknown territory without a survival kit, you should not venture into the spirit world without your psychic shields.

There are many ways in which you can further protect your psychic space or self. Here is another exercise for you to try during a full moon. You will need some fabric and a needle and thread, so that you can decorate a piece of cloth with the encircled rune of protection pictured at right.

This rune is specifically designed to protect your psychic self. You could include it on a bag for your divination tools, on a cushion on which you sit when you are doing your fortune-telling session, or on the cloth that you spread over your table before you set out your divination tools.

While constructing the bag, cushion, or tablecloth, visualize yourself within the rune design, finding peace and protection within the symbol. As you are stitching, say the following words:

> By this spell, this sacred charm,
> I'm free from danger, safe from harm,
> By this charm, this sacred spell,
> I bid my doubts and fears farewell.
>
> (LIAM CYFRIN)

Also visualize the energy from the earth flowing through your feet and into your hands, and the energy from the heavens flowing through your head and into your hands. Feel the clean, strong energy that your hands are imparting to your fabric and thread as you carry out your project. This will help increase the psychic strength of your work.

When you have finished the work, hang it out under the light of a full moon and say the above words to dedicate the cloth to your psychic protection.

ASTROLOGY

Many people have the misguided impression that astrology is a fairly simple craft to master. Every magazine and newspaper seems to have its own personal astrologer who predicts events for the day/week/month/year for each of the twelve zodiac signs. And although we all realize that these forecasts can only be a general calculation for each zodiac sign, these horoscopes are for a vast majority of readers a "must read" ritual.

Astrology, however, is a serious science that dates back many thousands of years. You need to fully understand the complexities of astrology before you can interpret a natal chart, even with the help of a computer program. For this, many years of study are required.

If you want to find out what your own natal chart says about you, first choose a reputable astrologer. He or she will require precise details of the time, date, and place of your birth. Your natal chart will be drawn up, and from this the astrologer will set about the task of "casting" your personal horoscope.

Your natal chart will provide you with important information about character traits—both positive and negative—that were imprinted upon you at birth. These characteristics will remain with you throughout your destiny, shaping your actions and decisions, unless you work on changing them; you may want to rid yourself of your negative aspects and strengthen your positive traits.

Astrology also shows what is possible and what is probable in all aspects of your life. You will discover the career path that will give you the most satisfaction and the personality type that will bring you the most joy in marriage.
Your prospects in terms of health, wealth, and happiness will be revealed, providing you with the ammunition you require to meet the challenges you are likely to encounter in your life. Such insight is priceless to your future well-being.

Although a complete analysis of how to use astrology for fortune-telling practices is beyond the scope of this dictionary, you can still use the information about a person's birthday and zodiac sign to understand that person's future. One way is to find out the person's zodiac number. Each of the twelve signs of the zodiac has an important number attached to it. The planetary influences, as represented by the zodiac number, have a strong influence on personality traits.

To find out your own zodiac number, use the table below to identify your zodiac sign and the number that zodiac sign resonates with.

ZODIAC SIGN	BIRTH DATES	PLANETARY INFLUENCE	ZODIAC NUMBER
Aries	March 21–April 20	Mars	9 (Nine)
Taurus	April 21–May 21	Venus	6 (Six)
Gemini	May 22–June 21	Mercury	5 (Five)
Cancer	June 22–July 22	Moon	2 (Two)
Leo	July 23–August 23	Sun	1 (One)
Virgo	August 24–September 22	Mercury	5 (Five)
Libra	September 23–October 23	Venus	6 (Six)
Scorpio	October 24–November 22	Mars	9 (Nine)
Sagittarius	November 23–December 21	Jupiter	3 (Three)
Capricorn	December 22–January 19	Saturn	8 (Eight)
Aquarius	January 20–February 18	Uranus	4 (Four)
Pisces	February 19–March 20	Neptune	7 (Seven)

DOES YOUR ZODIAC NUMBER MATCH
YOUR DESTINY NUMBER?

Find out your destiny number on page 100 and check on the following pages to see whether or not your destiny number and your zodiac number are compatible—this can make the difference between a smooth passage through life and a rough one.

An analysis of the combined influences of the destiny number and the zodiac number can provide valuable insight into a person's personality traits. It is both interesting and valuable to observe that fate, in its infinite wisdom, repeatedly pairs seemingly incompatible destiny and zodiac numbers—the solitary, intellectual Seven with the extroverted, frivolous Five, for instance. Is this fate's twisted sense of humor or its awareness that we need to share our talents with each other if we are to benefit from a lifetime of experience?

The following destiny number/zodiac number combinations can help you gain greater understanding of your child's personality, your partner's, and your own. With such understanding, many pitfalls can be avoided, and your life's journey can become a richer, more rewarding experience.

Destiny One/Zodiac One The personality with this powerful combination is indeed fortunate; there is enormous potential for growth, originality, and leadership here.

Destiny One/Zodiac Two Destiny One people are born to be leaders; however, the changeable vibration of the moon's influence on the usually focused One can make these people followers instead.

Destiny One/Zodiac Three This is a lucky combination: One is a natural-born hero, while Three showers blessings upon this person.

Destiny One/Zodiac Four The steadfast, hardworking Four influence on the One personality, who loves gain without pain, makes this a successful combination—these are the people who "make it happen."

Destiny One/Zodiac Five These personalities need constant challenges and are always looking for new experiences.

Destiny One/Zodiac Six Here is the megastar, with charm, beauty, and sensuality. One, the number of ambition, drive, and persistence, will bring the creativity of Six to fruition.

Destiny One/Zodiac Seven This is an incompatible combination, because the highly intelligent and gifted Seven loves privacy, while One wants center stage.

Destiny One/Zodiac Eight The aggressive, serious Saturn influence of Eight combined with the desire for power of One make this a successful but overpowering combination. Many politicians and other world leaders have this combination.

Destiny One/Zodiac Nine This can be an awesome combination. One loves to be loved in all ways, while Nine is highly sensual, so there is potential for an overly extroverted behavior pattern here.

Destiny Two/Zodiac One Timid Two and forceful One can hardly be called compatible, but unlike its counterpart Destiny One/Zodiac Two, the power of One will fight for supremacy in this combination.

Destiny Two/Zodiac Two This dreamer is too sensitive, too timid, and far too eager to please. A follower, this kindest, most gentle of personalities will likely succumb to peer pressure.

Destiny Two/Zodiac Three When the vivid imagination of Jupiter's influence is bestowed upon the timid Two personality, there can be great disillusion unless the person is encouraged to come down to earth often.

Destiny Two/Zodiac Four There is great potential for success in this combination because the hardworking, security-seeking influence of Four is a tremendous asset to the vivid imagination of Two.

Destiny Two/Zodiac Five The likelihood of risk-taking is evident in this combination, which gives us a careless personality who is easily bored and only too willing to meet trouble halfway.

Destiny Two/Zodiac Six These people have a lot of creative talent and believe in following their dreams. Their sensitive, sensual, and soft-hearted natures can also be taken advantage of, all too often leaving them broken-hearted—but only until the next time.

Destiny Two/Zodiac Seven Two/Seven people appear to march to the beat of a different drummer. Because they like to dream and intellectualize, they also like their own space and privacy.

Destiny Two/Zodiac Eight Serious, logical, analytical Eight does not combine well with the dreaming influence of Two, causing inner conflict. At best, the peace-making influence of Two will pacify this would-be perfectionist, resulting in a positive and powerful personality.

Destiny Two/Zodiac Nine Humanitarianism at its best will be the result of this combination. Two, who wishes to please, is an asset to Nine, a natural-born crusader for human rights.

Destiny Three/Zodiac One Versatile, talented Three combines with inventive One to ensure success for this personality.

Destiny Three/Zodiac Two This is a fun-loving combination. While they are fond of gossip, they have the advantage of possessing fewer faults than others. These personalities are highly creative and make good writers.

Destiny Three/Zodiac Three This combination is the ultimate in creativity. It is full of energy, extremely versatile, and highly intelligent. These people are restless and hyperactive, and can even be frivolous unless their goals are clearly defined.

Destiny Three/Zodiac Four This unconventional, anti-authoritarian combination often falls into trouble because of its rebellious nature. Practical, methodical, and patient, these people use their organizational skills to achieve success.

Destiny Three/Zodiac Five Travel, change, and new experiences are constants for this combination. These people are the Peter Pans of the universe—forever active, forever young at heart.

Destiny Three/Zodiac Six This is a lucky personality. As our world becomes busier, luck in love seems harder to find. But these people will find it, and their respect for and loyalty to family values will enrich their lives.

Destiny Three/Zodiac Seven Three's joyous Jupiter and the solitary nature of Seven would seem to make strange partners. People find this combination difficult to understand; in order to achieve success, this "odd couple" must learn to tolerate the differences in their needs.

Destiny Three/Zodiac Eight The cynical, analytical Eight influence on multitalented Three confers potential for success in several directions.

Destiny Three/Zodiac Nine This intuitive, sympathetic combination is quite compatible. Nine never stops in its quest to do good for humanity, and Three provides the energy and creativity necessary for these undertakings.

Destiny Four/Zodiac One The Builder (Four) plus the Inventor

(One) can create a rock-solid future for the owner of this personality combination.

Destiny Four/Zodiac Two Life was not meant to be easy for this combination: Four insists on commitment and Two panics at the very idea. People with this combination often seem to change their minds and moods.

Destiny Four/Zodiac Three Jupiter needs to convince the skeptical Four personality that its favors are well intended and permanent.

Destiny Four/Zodiac Four People of this serious-minded combination are reliable, trustworthy, honorable, and diligent, but they are also worriers and are confrontational.

Destiny Four/Zodiac Five These opposites need each other. When fate matches Four and Five, an interesting, talented individual seems to evolve, transforming this combination into a lovable personality.

Destiny Four/Zodiac Six These confident personalities ooze beauty, grace, and charm. They are attracted to the arts and their names can often be found in the credits of movies.

Destiny Four/Zodiac Seven Many musical and literary giants have this combination. The philosophical, solitary Seven does not object to the serious, hardworking Four, so when they are combined, others become the beneficiaries of their talents and dedication.

Destiny Four/Zodiac Eight This fearless combination is difficult to ignore, being strong-willed and strong-minded. These personalities are critical, analytical, logical, and honest.

Destiny Four/Zodiac Nine Though this combination of the solid, down-to-earth Four and the mystical, magical Nine appears incompatible, it is not, because earthy Four needs the compassion that Nine provides.

Destiny Five/Zodiac One The pioneering spirit of One complements the adventurous spirit of Five in this combination. New experiences are embraced and "challenge" becomes a key word.

Destiny Five/Zodiac Two This captivating combination loves an audience. These people are versatile, adaptable, and, like the chameleon, fit into any background. Their talent for the theatrical makes them popular.

Destiny Five/Zodiac Three Outrageous behavior is no stranger to this extroverted combination. These personalities have a great sense of humor and make good comedians.

9

Destiny Five/Zodiac Four Thrill-seeking Five and cautious, conservative Four make an incompatible combination that nevertheless invariably succeeds in accomplishing its goals and fulfilling its interesting, difficult karma.

Destiny Five/Zodiac Five These people are emotional and physical contortionists. Excessive behavior patterns are common among these extroverted, multitalented personalities.

4

Destiny Five/Zodiac Six A combination loaded with talent and blessed with a good personality. These people's entrepreneurial skills are evident from an early age. Witty and agreeable, they are very popular.

Destiny Five/Zodiac Seven This is a chaotic combination: the solitary, mysterious, sensitive Seven fails to inspire the fidgety Five to sort out its priorities. These personalities must learn tolerance if they are to operate effectively.

Destiny Five/Zodiac Eight The well-disciplined influence of Eight on the sometimes unruly Five is good, but too often logic robs this combination of sensitivity. These two industrious, self-motivated numbers make a good business combination, but must learn to relax.

Destiny Five/Zodiac Nine This dynamic combination is determined and relentless in its pursuit of good or evil. These people have more manipulative skills than any other number combination.

Destiny Six/Zodiac One Six aligned with One is a combination of intelligence and expansion. No mountain is too high, no goal unachievable.

Destiny Six/Zodiac Two Romantic, dreamy personalities evolve from this combination. These gentle folk are easygoing, laid-back, and imaginative.

Destiny Six/Zodiac Three This combination is versatile, creative, and generous. These personalities also have great imaginations.

Destiny Six/Zodiac Four Six personalities are loving and giving, and Fours can be found working hard for a living—together they are sensitive and reliable.

Destiny Six/Zodiac Five The creative, sensual Six influence combined with the acrobatic Five makes this a potentially winning combination.

Destiny Six/Zodiac Six This beautiful, romantic combination has a commitment to traditional family values. The welfare of others is a priority for them.

Destiny Six/Zodiac Seven The influence of Neptune, which covers dreams and fantasies, will have a resounding effect on Six's love of beauty and harmony, making these compatible.

Destiny Six/Zodiac Eight Sensitive Six personalities often find themselves in emotional torment when faced with the intolerant, critical Eight influence. Eight personalities are moralistic, with a strong code of ethics, whereas Six personalities exude spontaneity, making this combination difficult and incompatible.

Destiny Six/Zodiac Nine This combination lives to love. They are highly creative individuals who love the arts, nature, and humanity.

Destiny Seven/Zodiac One The organizational abilities of One are strong enough to persuade dreamy, elusive Seven to become focused and methodical, making this combination ambitious and confident in the pursuit of excellence.

Destiny Seven/Zodiac Two Illusion and imagination are strong in this combination, making these personalities good magicians.

Destiny Seven/Zodiac Three With the intellect of the Seven and the many talents of Three, this combination is advantaged from the beginning.

Destiny Seven/Zodiac Four The philosophical influence of Seven on the practical Four makes this combination a compatible duo. These people put enormous effort and energy into their goals, and they are often surprised to find themselves in the right place at the right time, just when they thought their efforts were futile.

Destiny Seven/Zodiac Five Philosophical Seven combined with the active, yet impatient, Five has people with this combination globe-trotting, either mentally or physically, for spiritual answers to their questions about the meaning of life.

Destiny Seven/Zodiac Six Spontaneous Six meets solitary Seven in this combination, yet these personalities can be most compatible, perhaps because of their mutual love of beauty, art, literature, and music.

Destiny Seven/Zodiac Seven Double Sevens are often psychically aware from an early age, so these people are attracted to all aspects of the occult—impressed by its good influences and compelled to investigate its dark side.

Destiny Seven/Zodiac Eight Eight knows exactly what it wants and how to get it, even if the road to success is hard and long. Seven is more inclined to review the situation over and over again. Inner conflict can be a result of this odd combination, causing mood changes.

Destiny Seven/Zodiac Nine Creative, artistic, psychic, humanitarian—all of these qualities are housed in this combination. These people prefer to work alone, behind the scenes. They are serious people who become totally absorbed in their quests.

Destiny Eight/Zodiac One Never say never and never give in to your weaknesses—so say these personalities, who are determined, focused, and dedicated.

Destiny Eight/Zodiac Two This combination produces personalities of a cautious and suspicious nature. The influence of logical Eight on passive Two can make these people difficult for others to understand.

Destiny Eight/Zodiac Three The influence of the energetic, versatile, and very creative Three on the hardworking, staid Eight personality does wonders for this combination. Though they are an odd couple, they need each other to create a balance.

Destiny Eight/Zodiac Four This winning combination is capable and reliable, but sometimes overly cautious. These people will achieve great things because of their dedication to hard work. Honest and tenacious, they have strong organizational abilities.

Destiny Eight/Zodiac Five Both these numbers love challenge and new experiences, but this is still a difficult personality combination to cope with. Five brings a sense of humor and adventure to the otherwise stoic, steadfast Eight.

Destiny Eight/Zodiac Six This is a real catch for someone looking for a partner in life. What better qualities could one wish for than those found in a loyal, trustworthy, dedicated, loving, and caring nature such as this?

Destiny Eight/Zodiac Seven Wanting and getting the best of all worlds seems to be the lifetime mission of people with this personality combination—a quest in which they are unstoppable.

Destiny Eight/Zodiac Eight This combination is all about excess. These personalities must learn to tolerate a destiny that they feel is too serious, too analytical, too practical, and too restrictive.

They are self-disciplined and focused, but also determined, stubborn, and strong-willed.

Destiny Eight/Zodiac Nine When you combine humanitarianism with common sense, the result is a responsible, caring personality who is able to assume a position of authority without becoming drunk with power. These personalities are courageous and compassionate.

Destiny Nine/Zodiac One These self-propelled personalities owe their competitive spirits to the Mars/Sun influence. They are indestructible in triumph but can be poor losers. They will spare no expense in achieving their goals.

Destiny Nine/Zodiac Two Personalities with this combination are good negotiators. The Nine/Two characteristics are an asset to careers such as marriage counseling and welfare work.

Destiny Nine/Zodiac Three Energetic and blessed with a good sense of humor and great wit, this is a lucky, multitalented combination.

Destiny Nine/Zodiac Four This combination is likely to have a short fuse. Nine/Four people are easily agitated, and this causes some erratic behavior patterns to develop. However, any success they achieve they have earned; they don't look for favors.

Destiny Nine/Zodiac Five Highly creative and energized, these personalities love challenge, change, and new experiences. They are quick to learn and quick to criticize.

Destiny Nine/Zodiac Six Beauty, harmony, and tranquility describe this combination; these personalities will do anything to have these qualities in their lives.

Destiny Nine/Zodiac Seven This personality combination is inspired and highly psychic. These people believe their mission in life is to find the secret of the afterlife. They have little or no regard for materialism, which causes them to mismanage their financial and material commitments.

Destiny Nine/Zodiac Eight People with this stubborn and determined combination will stop at nothing to achieve their goals. They are focused, diligent personalities who will work tirelessly for what they consider worthwhile.

Destiny Nine/Zodiac Nine This forceful, fiery combination produces personalities with character and courage. These people prefer to make their own rules and regulations, then follow them with gusto.

AURA READING

The technique of visualizing and interpreting auras is an advanced method of fortune-telling. Some psychics are born with this ability; others have mastered the technique by going to psychic workshops and developing their psychic powers.

Every living thing—plants, animals, and humans—has an energy field around it. This energy field is called an "aura," and those who can see and understand the various colors and levels of energy in an aura can therefore see the conditions of health, mood, and spiritual evolvement of the subject the aura surrounds.

In some psychic circles this technique is referred to as "overheading," because the reader looks only at the aura, not at the person's physical body.

The various colors of the aura reveal information that helps the reader detect positive and negative forces affecting the subject. The aura can also reveal areas of the body that are about to be attacked by illness, as well as those that have suffered previous attacks: the sensation felt when running the hands over the aura is distinctly colder when the vibrations of a past, present, or future injury—including, for example, a future car accident—are present.

Animals are very psychic beings, but they are not able to tell us where they are hurting when illness attacks them. However, a person who can read auras can detect these trouble spots by examining the animal's aura.

The power of evil can also be seen and felt in a person's aura. Should such a person reject an evil lifestyle, their aura heals and is soon clearly improved.

The diagnostic skills of a psychic healer can be invaluable in this area—is not prevention better than cure? Those working with a trained aura reader will benefit greatly.

AUTOMATIC WRITING

Automatic writing requires patience, meditation, and a serene atmosphere in which to work. It may not be the most popular method of fortune-telling, nor the easiest to master, but it is definitely a rewarding practice.

Mood music, incense burning, subdued lighting, and the gentle flicker of white candles are all psychic-enhancing ingredients useful to this exercise. Choose your favorite writing paper and a special pen, which you will then use solely for this purpose.

Select a comfortable straight-backed chair and let all tension go by taking some deep breaths. Place the pen in a relaxed position in your writing hand and you are ready to begin.

During this meditation phase, it helps if you can focus on a particular subject: for instance, your career, love life, finances, or even some current world event that interests you.

If you have chosen a person as your object of concentration, it would be advantageous for you to place a photograph of him or her in front of you. Imagine that someone else is controlling the pen and guiding it in your hand.

You may not be successful in getting a reaction in your first few attempts, but do not be disheartened. In time the pen will flow freely. In the early stages of your attempts, do not be surprised if the automatic writing is illegible and something of a scrawl—you may find sentence fragments, names, and single words. As you continue with your practice, you will be rewarded with clearer messages.

Some students of this craft are surprised to find that instead of the written text they were expecting to see, they are confronted by a drawing of a person or place connected with their inquiry. Sometimes, the first picture you create may turn out to be your spirit guide or guardian angel (see pages 84–91).

CHINESE HOROSCOPE

In Western astrology, the month in which a person was born is believed to determine that person's general destiny and character traits. In Chinese astrology, it is the *year* that is believed to have this kind of effect on a person's fate.

The Chinese believe in the Great Year, a twelve-year cycle in which each year has a particular energy that affects aspects of the lives of those born in that year: the turn of events, the personality, and aspects such as luck and prosperity.

By the eighth or ninth century A.D., this set of beliefs included a group of twelve animals, each of which was believed to epitomize the qualities of one of the twelve years in the Great Year cycle. The first year is the Year of the Rat and the twelfth is the Year of the Pig. Each year in the cycle also has a particular energy concerning business and finances.

The year in the Great Cycle during which a person is born is a year in which the person will enjoy good fortune each time it recurs—those born in the Year of the Dragon will find that they have particularly prosperous times during subsequent Years of the Dragon, for example.

To find out what animal sign you are, check the table on pages 78–79, and see which period your birthday falls in and what animal influences future years.

YEAR OF THE RAT
2/19/1996 to 2/6/1997 • 2/7/2008 to 2/1/2009

As the Year of the Rat is the beginning of a new twelve-year cycle, this year promises opportunities to start new ventures and

 businesses. This is the time to sow the seeds for future prosperity. It is an auspicious time for the Rat, Tiger, Dragon, Snake, Monkey, and Dog, but a potentially troublesome time for the Hare, Sheep, Rooster, and Pig.

YEAR OF THE OX

1/7/1997 to 1/27/1998 • 1/26/2009 to 2/13/2010

Develop the projects you started last year or consolidate your position. This is not a good time to start new ventures unless you are able to complete them within the same year. Investigate stable

investments and do not go into risky propositions. This is a year of stability. It is an auspicious time for the Rat, Ox, Snake, and Pig, but a potentially troublesome time for the Tiger, Hare, Dragon, Sheep, and Dog.

YEAR OF THE TIGER

1/28/1998 to 2/15/1999 • 2/14/2010 to 2/2/2011

This is an unpredictable year, when success is assured for only a few, such as those who were born in the Year of the Tiger. It is a year of upheavals and changes—wars and financial turbulence can occur in this year. It is best not

to enter into any risky ventures and to be prepared for unexpected turns, although not necessarily for the worse. It is an auspicious time for the Rat, Ox, Tiger, Hare, Dragon, Horse, and Dog, but a potentially troublesome time for the Snake, Monkey, and Pig.

YEAR OF THE HARE

2/16/1999 to 2/4/2000 • 2/3/2011 to 1/22/2012

This is a peaceful and stable year, with opportunities arising for joint ventures and the further development of business ideas. It is a time for consolidation and for strengthening your financial position. The aggression of the Tiger Year is counterbalanced by the return of harmony and peace usually signaled by the Hare Year. It is an auspicious time for the Ox, Hare, Snake, Dog, and Pig, but a potentially troublesome time for the Rat, Dragon, Monkey, and Rooster.

ANCIENT WISDOM

If you see a well-fed rat unexpectedly turn up in your home, take it as a sign of future prosperity.

YEAR OF THE DRAGON

2/5/2000 to 1/23/2001 • 1/23/2012 to 2/9/2013

The time is ripe for the start of adventurous and imaginative business plans. This is a year of great ups and downs on a worldwide basis. If you are able to tap into the fire energy of this year, you will benefit tremendously. However, never turn your back to fire or you may get burned! It is an auspicious time for the Rat, Tiger, Dragon, Snake, and Horse, but a potentially troublesome time for the Ox, Hare, and Sheep.

YEAR OF THE SNAKE

1/24/2001 to 2/11/2002 • 2/10/2013 to 1/30/2014

Watching your back in finance and business is the key to survival this year. This is not a good time to start any new ventures. There is often great political instability in these years, and upheavals such as earthquakes and other natural disasters. Be cautious, and watch out for any potential takeover bids in your business or the emergence of

 a serious competitor in your business sphere. It is an auspicious time for the Ox, Hare, Snake, Sheep, and Rooster, but a potentially troublesome time for the Rat, Ox, Tiger, Monkey, Dog, and Pig.

YEAR OF THE HORSE

2/12/2002 to 1/31/2003 • 1/31/2014 to 2/18/2015

This is a year of surprises and large-scale changes, a good time for expansion. This is a good year to make those changes to your personal and business life that will help it grow and expand. It is an auspicious time for the Tiger, Dragon, Horse, Sheep, and Dog, but a potentially troublesome time for the Rat, Ox, Hare, and Rooster.

YEAR OF THE SHEEP

2/1/2003 to 1/21/2004 • 2/19/2015 to 2/7/2016

In contrast with the Year of the Horse, this year is one of quiet contemplation, nurture, and consolidation. This is the time when long-term differences can be reconciled and when your years of toil will be rewarded. This is the harvest year. It is an auspicious time for the Hare, Dragon, Sheep, Rooster, and Pig, but a potentially troublesome time for the Ox, Dragon, Monkey, and Dog.

YEAR OF THE MONKEY

1/22/2004 to 2/8/2005 • 2/8/2016 to 1/27/2017

This is a very uncertain time, with unpredictability being the key word. Investors should look into diversifying their finances. Traditional organizations may experience problems, while new career and business opportunities may become available. It is a year to move ahead and investigate new possibilities. It is an auspicious time for the Rat, Dragon, Horse, Monkey, Rooster, and Dog, but a potentially troublesome time for the Tiger, Hare, and Pig.

YEAR OF THE ROOSTER

2/9/2005 to 1/28/2006 • 1/28/2017 to 2/15/2018

There will be a general feeling of agitation this year, and some businesses will experience a number of reversals while others, particularly in fashion or luxury businesses, will prosper. The year will herald a new awareness of yourself—your strengths and weaknesses, which will help you forge ahead in the years to come. It is an auspicious time for the Ox, Snake, Sheep, Monkey, Rooster, and Pig, but a potentially troublesome time for the Rat, Tiger, and Hare.

YEAR OF THE DOG

1/29/2006 to 2/17/2007 • 2/16/2018 to 2/4/2019

Loyalty in business and resistance to takeovers is a major feature of this year. This year focuses on the family and provides you with an opportunity to strengthen your family and/or family business base. It is an auspicious time for the Tiger, Horse, Monkey, Dog, and Pig, but a potentially troublesome time for the Dragon and Snake.

YEAR OF THE PIG

2/18/2007 to 2/6/2008 • 2/5/2019 to 1/24/2020

Business activity during this year may be rather slow. This is a good time to bring to a close any long-term ventures. Start planning for new long-term ventures this year, but wait until the start of the new

cycle in the next year—the Year of the Rat—to begin them. It is an auspicious time for the Ox, Hare, Sheep, Dog, and Pig, but a potentially troublesome time for the Rat, Tiger, Dragon, Snake, and Monkey.

TABLE OF CHINESE ASTROLOGY CYCLES:
WHICH ANIMAL ARE YOU?

The table below outlines the years that correspond to a particular animal. By knowing which animal resonates with your birthday, you can see which years will be beneficial to you (see pages 74–77). You may also wish to work with the image of your animal in good luck charms or amulets of protection.

RAT	HARE
February 5, 1924–January 24, 1925	February 2, 1927–January 22, 1928
January 24, 1936–February 10, 1937	February 19, 1939–February 7, 1940
February 10, 1948–January 28, 1949	February 6, 1951–January 26, 1952
January 28, 1960–February 14, 1961	January 25, 1963–February 12, 1964
February 15, 1972–February 2, 1973	February 11, 1975–January 30, 1976
February 2, 1984–February 19, 1985	January 29, 1987–February 16, 1988
February 19, 1996–February 6, 1997	February 16, 1999–February 4, 2000

OX	DRAGON
January 25, 1925–February 12, 1926	January 23, 1928–February 9, 1929
February 11, 1937–January 30, 1938	February 8, 1940–January 26, 1941
January 29, 1949–February 16, 1950	January 27, 1952–February 13, 1953
February 15, 1961–February 4, 1962	February 13, 1964–February 1, 1965
February 3, 1973–January 22, 1974	January 31, 1976–February 17, 1977
February 20, 1985–February 8, 1986	February 17, 1988–February 5, 1989
February 7, 1997–January 27, 1998	February 5, 2000–January 23, 2001

TIGER	SNAKE
February 13, 1926–February 1, 1927	February 10, 1929–January 29, 1930
January 31, 1938–February 18, 1939	January 27, 1941–February 14, 1942
February 17, 1950–February 5, 1951	February 14, 1953–February 2, 1954
February 5, 1962–January 24, 1963	February 2, 1965–January 20, 1966
January 23, 1974–February 10, 1975	February 18, 1977–February 6, 1978
February 9, 1986–January 28, 1987	February 6, 1989– January 26, 1990
January 28, 1998–February 15, 1999	January 24, 2001–February 11, 2002

HORSE

January 30, 1930–February 16, 1931
February 15, 1942–February 4, 1943
February 3, 1954–January 23, 1955
January 21, 1966–February 8, 1967
February 7, 1978–January 27, 1979
January 27, 1990–February 14, 1991
February 12, 2002–January 31, 2003

ROOSTER

January 26, 1933–February 13, 1934
February 13, 1945–February 1, 1946
January 31, 1957–February 17, 1958
February 17, 1969–February 5, 1970
February 5, 1981–January 24, 1982
January 23, 1993–February 9, 1994
February 9, 2005– January 28, 2006

SHEEP

February 17, 1931–February 5, 1932
February 5, 1943–January 24, 1944
January 24, 1955–February 11, 1956
February 9, 1967–January 29, 1968
January 28, 1979–February 15, 1980
February 15, 1991–February 3, 1982
February 1, 2003–January 21, 2004

DOG

February 14, 1934–February 3, 1935
February 2, 1946–January 21, 1947
February 18, 1958–February 7, 1959
February 6, 1970–January 26, 1971
January 25, 1982–February 12, 1983
February 10, 1994–January 30, 1995
January 29, 2006–February 17, 2007

MONKEY

February 6, 1932–January 25, 1933
January 25, 1944–February 12, 1945
February 12, 1956–January 30, 1957
January 30, 1968–February 16, 1969
February 16, 1980–February 4, 1981
February 4, 1992–January 22, 1993
January 22, 2004–February 8, 2005

PIG

February 4, 1935–January 23, 1936
January 22, 1947–February 9, 1948
February 8, 1959–January 27, 1960
January 27, 1971–February 14, 1972
February 13, 1983–February 1, 1984
January 31, 1995–February 18, 1996
February 18, 2007–February 6, 2008

■ FOR **COFFEE GROUND READING**,
SEE **TEA-LEAF READING**, ON PAGES 178–183.

CRYSTAL BALL

Fortune-telling by way of crystal ball gazing is another method that is best served by good meditation skills and the benefit of a psychic-enhancing environment.

A good-quality crystal ball is an expensive item, but it is a good investment because of its beautiful appearance and hardiness—and it can be a "once-in-a-lifetime" purchase. It is a popular practice of fortune-tellers to keep their crystal covered with a velvet cloth when it is not being used, so that it does not attract negative or disruptive energies and is not touched by sunlight.

It is important that you practice crystal ball gazing in your special psychic space, as you are opening yourself psychically for visions to come to you and you will need to concentrate very hard, particularly while learning this skill.

Formulate a clear and unambiguous question that you wish to have answered by your crystal ball visions. While meditating on your reasons for the consultation, place your hands around the crystal, without touching it, and feel the energy surrounding it.

You will begin to have impressions about incidents relating to your inquiry. These impressions will take shape as visions or symbols that appear within the crystal. By using this method of fortune-telling you are employing and improving your clairvoyant skills. By the time you have mastered this craft, you will be receiving detailed and accurate accounts about events connected to the person whose destiny is being predicted.

Crystal ball gazing is a little like watching a silent movie—you see images that move but you don't hear anything. It is a pleasant and informative pastime as well as a serious method of fortune-telling; however, since life is not always a barrel of laughs, you will occasionally see a picture predicting a sad occasion. Should you tell? If you need to ask yourself this question, the answer is *no*.

Usually crystal balls are clear quartz crystal or obsidian. Once you have purchased your crystal ball, wash it under running water and pat it dry with a clean cloth, either black or white. Purify the stone by leaving it in a position where the light of a full moon will reach it.

CRYSTAL BALL MEDITATION: STEP BY STEP

1 Decide what question you would like to have answered. If you are merely practicing, consider asking the crystal ball for the location of an item that you have lost. Make the question as simple as possible. Some fortune-tellers ask their friends and clients to write down on a piece of paper the question they seek to have answered. The crystal ball is then rested on top of the piece of paper to enhance the accuracy of the answer.

2 Sit in front of the crystal ball and let your mind go blank. This is sometimes the hardest thing to do. Consider doing a personal cleansing (see pages 56–57) before using this technique—that way you will already have spent some time stilling your thoughts in the bath. You could also consider concentrating on your breathing while you gaze (but not stare) at your crystal ball.

3 As your mind stills, the crystal will seem to be filling with a slight mist or swirls. Do not try to focus on the patterns that are starting to appear. Simply note their appearance. As your eyes become accustomed to this way of "seeing," these pictures and symbols will start to grow in strength and clarity, allowing you to interpret the images in terms of the question you have asked the ball. Some fortune-tellers use dream symbols to interpret the images they see, but it is up to you to determine if there is a source of inspiration that helps you understand what the pictures mean. When you keep an open mind, the images' meanings will come to you.

DICE

When dice become instruments of fortune-telling, it's a case of "short question, quick answer"—it is the method of divination that is fastest and easiest to learn. The only piece of equipment you need for this practice, apart from the three dice used for throwing, is a large piece of cardboard. Draw a circle in white chalk on the cardboard. Evening is said to be the most favorable time for this practice, as it is traditionally the calmest part of the day. A superstition says that if you use this fortune-telling technique during an electrical storm your predictions will be unreliable.

Method 1

Place the three dice in a small box or dish. Close your eyes, make a wish, and then toss the dice onto the board. Dice that fall outside the circle should not be counted. Add up the number of dots on the dice within the circle and interpret the total figure using this chart.

Three	Imminent good luck and a wish fulfilled.
Four	A slight setback will cause disappointment.
Five	A stranger brings much new happiness.
Six	A new blessing comes well disguised.
Seven	You will become the victim of gossip.
Eight	Confusion causes unwise decisions—don't act in haste.
Nine	Success in love and reconciliations.
Ten	Success in career and finance is imminent.
Eleven	Short-term illness causes you anxiety.
Twelve	Seek advice regarding legal documents.
Thirteen	Self-pity causes delays and hassles.
Fourteen	A new social circle brings excitement.
Fifteen	Follow your intuition about false friends.
Sixteen	A short journey brings profit and pleasure.
Seventeen	A stranger from overseas brings successful propositions.
Eighteen	Happiness, financial success, and a rise in status.

Method 2

For this method, only two dice are used. Place the dice in a small box or bowl and shake them well. At the same time, make a silent wish for a good future. Toss the dice onto a flat surface and interpret the combination by referring to the table below.

Six six	A period of general success starts with a financial gain.
Six five	Your help with a charitable organization receives recognition and reward.
Six four	A bitter dispute is resolved in a court of law.
Six three	A short journey will end with an unexpected pleasant surprise.
Six two	Someone gives you a gift that is unusual but useful.
Six one	Emotional problems you are experiencing will soon be sorted out.
Five five	A change of address and a new social circle are overdue.
Five four	You will make a sizeable profit from a small investment.
Five three	Unexpected visitors and happy reunions will surprise you.
Five two	A friend discovers she is pregnant with twins.
Five one	A fiery love affair suffers early burnout.
Four four	Neighbors hold a noisy party and forget to invite you.
Four three	You are "borrowing sorrow from tomorrow," worrying about trivia.
Four two	Beware of flattery from a handsome but fickle admirer.
Four one	Finances take a dive, but only for a short period.
Three three	Rivalry in your love life causes jealous outbursts.
Three two	Don't gamble today unless you are prepared to lose.
Three one	Someone else's misfortune turns out to be your gain.
Two two	A new love affair is the beginning of long-term happiness.
Two one	An article of sentimental value is lost but will turn up later.
One one	Important decisions made now will result in success.

G

GUARDIAN ANGELS

WHAT ARE GUARDIAN ANGELS
AND SPIRIT GUIDES?

The choice of name—spirit guide or guardian angel—is personal.
Some believe that the spirit beings who watch over us are angels,
and prefer to call their own spirit guide a "guardian angel."

For hundreds of years it was thought by many people that
the use of a Ouija board was the simplest and fastest way to
communicate with their spirit guides. However, the entities you
contact through these means, regardless of their claims, are never
your deceased relative or your guardian angel or spirit guide; they
are disembodied entities from the nether regions of the spirit world,
and no matter how accurate they sometimes appear to be, they can
be malicious and ultimately dangerous.

Communication with your guardian angel
will not come about if your pursuit of psychic
development is for the wrong reasons or you
don't treat it with respect. If you want to develop
a mutual understanding with your guardian
angel, you will need to commit to the process of
serious psychic development (see pages 18–61).
Your guardian angel looks after your well-being,
so pay it the respect it deserves by frequently
thinking of it with love and thanking it whenever
it assists you.

If you allow your communication skills to
become more finely tuned, you will discover that
there are many instances when your guardian
angel intervenes on your behalf to bring about a
favorable outcome regarding romantic, business,
or health issues. We tend to keep our guardian
angels very much on their spiritual toes with our
petty grievances.

THE ROLE OF A GUARDIAN ANGEL

The main role of your guardian angel is to assist you in your spiritual development and to protect you from danger, if that is appropriate, or at least warn you of it—but you need to listen to those warnings. They usually come in the form of a strong intuitive feeling. People occasionally report that their survival of a near-fatal accident was accompanied by a glimpse of their guardian angel.

Guardian angels are highly evolved spirits who understand that as long as you are living on a material planet, you need to learn material values as well as spiritual values. They are here to help you balance the material with the spiritual. They respect the fact that you have free will and will make important decisions and choices yourself, and though they may tug at your conscience when you flirt with danger, they understand that you must learn through experience.

Guardian angels have no desire to intrude upon your privacy. It is not the role of guardian angels to judge your lifestyle, nor is it their job to decide your beliefs. The more you respect your guardian angel, the more it will help you.

Your guardian angel will enlist the help of other specialist angels or "devas" (the Indian word for angels that is now commonly used in the West) when necessary. These angels were created as angels; many guardian angels were once human beings. The angels or devas specialize in healing or in helping people or plants grow. There is an angel for everything you do that might require help. Guardian angels ask the specialist angels to help them in their tasks.

The term "guardian angel" may conjure up visual impressions of ethereal beings, but if and when you ever see yours, you may be surprised to discover how ordinary it looks. The important thing is to believe and trust in the work guardian angels do on your behalf. And remember, they are not simply invisible welfare workers.

WHAT IS AN ANGEL?

While there is a popular notion of angels sitting on clouds and playing harps with beatific expressions, angels are in fact workers, just like humans. Their mission is to guide all living beings toward the "light" of which they are a part.

HOW TO RECOGNIZE YOUR GUARDIAN ANGEL

Guardian angels rarely make their presence known through ghostly apparitions. They can be quite creative and even comical in finding ways to get your attention. They may use a distinct signal as their calling card. For instance, if you always hear a buzzing sound in your ears or in your head just before you receive a premonition, you will soon identify that sound with your guardian angel.

Other common signals are: a churning feeling in your stomach, the hairs standing up on the back of your neck, a sudden gust of wind brushing against your face when there is no breeze, and objects not being in their usual place and then turning up safely in the least likely place.

Though very few people see apparitions, those who can should recognize the difference between their guardian angel and a haunting spirit. A chilled atmosphere accompanies haunting entities or poltergeists, and you will feel frightened. A cool breeze will arrive with your guardian angel, and your guardian angel instills peace and comfort, even as it is trying to attract your attention.

Occasionally your guardian angel might try to attract your attention by doing things that could frighten you. For example, it might knock the telephone receiver off the hook a couple of times or change the TV channel or even turn the TV on and off. These funny little incidents happen only when you have forgotten to do something important, and unlike similar incidents caused by poltergeists, they will stop as soon as you have remembered what you were supposed to do or where you were supposed to be at the time.

The loving energy emitted by guardian angels is palpable to those who are open to receiving it and is one of the most powerful signs of their existence in our lives, creating a feeling of protection in times of fear or danger and a calming reassurance in times of self-doubt.

BUILDING A RELATIONSHIP WITH
YOUR GUARDIAN ANGEL

Once you have accepted the fact that you have a guardian angel, the next important step is to find a way to communicate with it so that you can build a happy and satisfactory relationship. This friendship deserves the same respect and appreciation as any other kind of relationship.

Good relationships prosper with good communication skills and are nourished by the quality time invested in them. You must ask yourself how much energy you are willing to contribute to this relationship. Naturally, it takes more time and effort to build up a relationship with someone who lives in a far-off land and speaks a different language. It is not easy to overcome these barriers, but anyone who has tried can tell you that it is worth it.

Acknowledgment, trust, respect, and loyalty are the words that should guide you in your quest to achieve a compatible and lasting bond with your guardian angel. It is essential that you understand the importance of these qualities when you set out to achieve what is, in effect, priceless.

Begin each day with a simple greeting as an acknowledgment of your guardian angel's presence. If you feel inclined, wear an angel pendant or pin as a statement of your belief and faith in guardian angels. Also, pledge your trust each day by chanting a short silent affirmation. For example:

Guardian angel, in whom I trust, guide my actions today.

As a sign of respect, spend two or three minutes at the end of each day meditating on the emotional security you have because of the loving relationship between you and your guardian angel. Pledge your loyalty to this union by lighting two white candles while you chant an affirmation such as:

Guardian angel, I acknowledge your presence in my life
and I trust the guidance you offer me.

COMMUNICATING WITH GUARDIAN ANGELS

There have been reports of people who, during a dramatic escape from death by accident, have glimpsed a being made of light intervening in the situation. However, the most common means guardian angels use to communicate with us are through our own intuition, appearing to us in dreams or, occasionally, sending a strong voice inside our heads.

What is the difference between an angel voice and the voices people with mental illnesses hear? When an angel speaks to you inside your head, it is always good and loving, and it occurs only during an emergency or other very serious situation. This means that it is very rare indeed. A person would be lucky to have one such incident in his or her life.

When you are communicating with your guardian angel, it is important and rewarding to develop your own system of exercises. Simplicity and sincerity are the main components in gaining a continuous flow of communication with your guardian angel.

Affirmations that are easily committed to memory are a good way to acknowledge your guardian angel and express your desire to work with it, so that you may learn and be guided by its advice in times of confusion and important life-altering decisions. Affirmations are also a wonderful way to show your guardian angel your appreciation for all that it is doing for you.

Taking the trouble to create affirmations, such as the one below, and then vocalizing them during a specific time each day, will reap untold reward from your guardian angel, because in this way you are demonstrating respect.

> *Guardian angel, who takes care of me in good times*
> *and in bad,*
> *Who tries to dissuade me from foolish choices, and*
> *Who consoles me when I'm sad,*
> *I wish to say thank you for choosing me to watch over*
> *and protect.*
> *May I gain the wisdom to know that your advice*
> *Must be used for good cause and effect.*

AFFIRMATIONS OF RESPECT AND PROTECTION
FOR YOUR GUARDIAN ANGEL

Affirmations that demonstrate acceptance and recognition of the important role your guardian angel plays in your life can become a vital part of developing and maintaining your relationship with your guardian angel. Try the following exercise.

This exercise requires a positive and serene attitude and ambience; the latter can be evoked by lighting two white candles—these represent the white light of protection that will flow between you and your guardian angel—playing some relaxing mood music, and setting up an oil burner or a bowl of hot water into which you pour seven drops of essential oil.

Breathe in and out slowly until you are relaxed, then breathe normally. Now meditate on your guardian angel's presence. When you are ready, chant the following affirmation three times:

> *I recognize and appreciate my guardian angel, and*
> *I do pledge to accept the guidance and*
> *Listen to the advice of this divine messenger*
> *That is given with love and compassion*
> *Without malice, mischief, or other negative energy.*

DISTINGUISHING BETWEEN A DECEASED LOVED ONE
AND YOUR GUARDIAN ANGEL

Some people become confused about the difference between encounters with guardian angels and encounters with deceased loved ones. Very few people ever actually see their guardian angels, whereas almost everyone sees a deceased loved one, either in dreams or in that time between being asleep and being awake. The deceased loved one usually only wishes to comfort and reassure his or her grieving family and to let them know that he or she is now supremely happy and not suffering in any way.

The inner peace and happiness that the deceased loved one generates is sometimes so intense and unforgettable that it leaves the grieving person with the same degree of comfort and protection as that provided by a guardian angel. This leads to the belief that the deceased loved one has now become this person's new guardian angel. Your guardian angel will understand this and will help you understand the true nature of your encounter.

WHEN A GUARDIAN ANGEL APPEARS
IN YOUR DREAMS

The most documented method of
guardian angels communicating with
their people is through dreams.
Religious writings, including the Bible,
and myth are full of accounts of
guardian angel communication using
the medium of dreams. There are
certain signs that identify the being you
are speaking with (or listening to) in
your dream as your guardian angel.

First, your guardian angel will always
take the form of someone for whom you
have the highest respect, and throughout the communication you
will feel surrounded by love, even if you are suffering extreme
anguish.

The second indication is that your guardian angel will speak to
you with great kindness. The voice will be clear and the message
one of simple wisdom that will show you how to extricate yourself
from the problem or sadness that you are experiencing.

Whenever you want to seek specific advice from your guardian
angel on a matter that is important to you, decide to have a meeting
with your guardian angel while you sleep. Some people will be
successful right away, while others may need to practice conscious
dreaming for a while before they remember a meeting.

If you have difficulty remembering your dreams, try keeping a
journal or notebook beside your bed, and as soon as you wake up,
record any fragments you can remember.

Before you go to sleep, clear your mind of all your everyday
concerns and think only of seeing your guardian angel. Lie
comfortably in your bed and imagine that you are being led by a
white light to a beautiful space. Say the following words:

This is my moment, my time of great joy
My time of dreaming which naught shall annoy
Guardian angel stay close by my side
Be my companion, my staff, and my guide.

WHEN A GUARDIAN ANGEL SPEAKS TO YOU
THROUGH YOUR INTUITION

Everyone has intuition, but it is very difficult these days to hear it,
let alone trust it, when our technological world is telling us that
there is no such thing or that what we think of as intuition is really
just our imaginations working overtime.

In early times, and in the world of nature, intuition could mean
the difference between life and death. For us, listening to our
intuition will mean the difference between a life lived on the surface
and one that is multidimensional.

Before you can trust your intuition and hear your angel speaking
to you, you will need to be able to distinguish your intuition from
your fears or desires. When your intuition is at work, or when your
angel is speaking to you through it, you are conscious of receiving
some information that you know to be true. There is a sense of

peace about this knowledge. It feels like
something that originated outside
yourself. The information may cause
you distress or great joy, but there is a
sense of quiet behind whatever other
emotions you experience as a result of
the message—in fact, your response to
your intuition is similar to your
response when you learn something
important, something which you know
to be true, from another individual.

If your certainty about an issue is
a result of your own hopes and fears,
rather than your angel's advice, there
may be a sense of desperation behind your joyfulness. Such a
feeling of disquiet will never accompany an angel encounter. You
need to learn to "hear" this underlying feeling so that you can tell
whether the message you have received comes from your angel
or yourself.

See pages 28–31 for information about unlocking and developing
your intuition.

I

I CHING

One of the five classics of Chinese
antiquity, the *I Ching*, or *Book of Changes*, is
an oracle that you can consult to guide you
through every aspect of your life. While
many people believe it is a form of fortune-
telling, its purpose is to show you how to
handle difficult situations, make wise
decisions, and clarify the truth.

The *I Ching* is based on the belief that
the future develops in accordance with fixed laws, according to
calculable numbers. If these numbers are known, future events can
be "calculated." The *I Ching* attributes numbers to the earth and to
heaven—the even numbers are assigned to the world of earth and
the uneven numbers to heaven. And, interestingly, like Pythagoras,
the *I Ching* attributes the feminine (yin) to even numbers and the
masculine (yang) to uneven numbers.

The *I Ching* is made up of sixty-four hexagrams, which relate to
all aspects of daily life. The hexagrams are thought to have been
worked out by the founder of the Chou dynasty, Wen Wang, in the
twelfth century B.C. Commentaries were written, around 475–221
B.C., for each hexagram. Modern translations of these commentaries
take different forms, so when you buy a copy of the *I Ching*, check
all the translations available to see which you prefer. For instance,
the James Legge translation separates the hexagrams from the
commentaries, while the Richard Wilhelm translation puts the
commentaries and the hexagrams together. Another difference
between these two translations is that Legge did not translate the
names of the hexagrams while Richard Wilhelm did—the English
names used in this book are from the Wilhelm translation.

But whatever translation you choose, the concept is the same.
The *I Ching* is concerned with the cycle of change caused by action
and reaction.

THE NATURE OF THE ORACLE

If you are sincere when you throw coins or count out yarrow sticks seeking an answer to something, the *I Ching* will try very hard to help you. If you are insincere, the *I Ching* will give you either a scolding or a meaningless hexagram—the oracle will not be bothered with tests or games. If you are not content with the answer the *I Ching* gives you, because it is not what you wanted to hear (the *I Ching* is more concerned with truth and honor than with making you feel better), and continue to ask the same question again and again, you will no doubt get hexagram 4, Meng (Youthful Folly). Youthful Folly is very much the scolding parent.

The *I Ching* teaches you to consider the consequences of your actions and the way you think about things. It requires you to scrutinize your motives and attitudes, and to strive to strengthen your character. If you are behaving in a weak manner, the oracle will refer to "the inferior man."

If you wish to build your character and develop spiritually, the *I Ching* will work wonders for you—before too long, you will find yourself thinking in the way of the *I Ching*.

THE TRIGRAMS

The trigrams, which are formed by three lines that are either broken or unbroken, are immensely important symbols; they are the basis of the ancient philosophy of China, the building blocks of the *I Ching*. It was believed that the legendary emperor Fu Hsi, in the twenty-fourth century B.C., saw these patterns on the back of a tortoise. Each trigram corresponds to the dynamics of many aspects of life, such as the landscape, personality types, family members, and the animal kingdom.

TRIGRAM		PERSONALITY	LANDSCAPE	FAMILY	ANIMAL
Ch'ien	☰	The Creative	Heaven	Strong	Horse
K'un	☷	The Receptive	Earth	Yielding	Cow
Chen	☳	The Arousing	Thunder	Movement	Dragon
Ken	☶	Keeping Still	Mountain	Standstill	Dog
K'an	☵	The Abysmal	Water	Dangerous	Pig
Li	☲	The Clinging	Fire	Dependence	Pheasant
Tui	☱	The Joyous	Lake	Pleasure	Sheep
Sun	☴	The Gentle	Wood	Penetrating	Cock

Constructing the hexagrams

The hexagrams are a stack of six broken and unbroken lines; the lines are a combination of any two of the trigrams. There are sixty-four possible combinations that can be made with the eight basic trigrams. These combinations are the key to finding guidance for your problem through the *I Ching*—the oracle is divided into sixty-four sections.

To access the wisdom of the hexagram appropriate to your question, you must learn how to construct each line, finding out whether each line is broken or unbroken.

One of the many ways of consulting the *I Ching* is to throw a coin six times and note each time whether it falls heads or tails. If you have thrown heads, this corresponds with yang energy, which means an unbroken line. If you have thrown tails, this corresponds with yin energy, which means a broken line:

——————— heads (yang energy)

— — tails (yin energy)

Sit in a quiet place and think of a question for which you wish to consult the *I Ching*, such as "What is stopping me from being prosperous?" Focus on the coin you wish to use. You may have a lucky coin that you wish to use (either Western or Eastern in origin) for this purpose. Throw the coin six times and write down the results, adding each result above the previous one.

Start at the bottom of your stack and write down whether you have a broken or unbroken line for each of the six levels. You should have something like this:

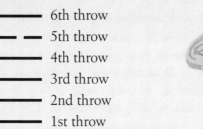

——————— 6th throw

— — 5th throw

——————— 4th throw

——————— 3rd throw

——————— 2nd throw

——————— 1st throw

Each hexagram in the *I Ching* has a number. Consult the table opposite to find out the number of the hexagram that you have tossed. Look again at your hexagram and note the configuration of the top three lines. Find the match in the upper horizontal line of the table below. Now look at the bottom three lines of your hexagram and find a match in the vertical line. Trace a line down from your top line and across from your side line to find the number of your hexagram. In the example above, the number would be 14.

HEXAGRAM TABLE

LOWER \ UPPER	☰	☳	☵	☶	☷	☴	☲	☱
☰	1	11	34	5	26	9	14	43
☷	12	2	16	8	23	20	35	45
☳	25	24	51	3	27	42	21	17
☵	6	7	40	29	4	59	64	47
☶	33	15	62	39	52	53	56	31
☴	44	46	32	48	18	57	50	28
☲	13	36	55	63	22	37	30	49
☱	10	19	54	60	41	61	38	58

Once you have found out the number, consult the table on the next page to understand its advice.

It is not always a good time to consult the *I Ching*. Chinese seers throw two wooden pieces, which are curved on one side and flat on the other, to determine whether it is a good time to use the *I Ching*. The two pieces are thrown three times: if on each throw both land with the flat side up, it is best to consult the *I Ching* at another time.

For people who use the *I Ching* sincerely on a regular basis, it does indeed seem to be the ultimate parent—all-knowing, all-wise, compassionate, and scolding. It seems to have genuine emotions and a forceful living presence. The *I Ching* will never let a sincere person down. All the hexagrams give powerful lessons.

Interpreting the hexagrams

The text of the *I Ching* is highly symbolic and can be very difficult to understand. It is important to realize that the interpretation of the imagery requires you to stretch your mind over the hexagram and let it float over the imagery, without judgment, to see how it affects your situation. For instance, hexagram 7, Shih (the Army), can refer to a group of many or few people that would benefit by operating in a manner similar to that of an army; this could mean your place of work, a club you belong to—any group, in fact, that needs order, a leader, loyalty, and support in order to get past difficulties. This same hexagram could also be referring to your mind. If you are being overwhelmed by your problems, your mind could need ordering; this hexagram shows you how to set your personal chaos in order.

The *I Ching* is a complex, lyrical method of divination that has been simplified over the years to make it widely accessible.

NUMBER AND MEANING	
1	Have faith in the plans you have already made.
2	Do not force the issue; wait for the right time.
3	Allow the issue to germinate further.
4	Great future promised but be patient now.
5	Great success but you will need to bide your time and not force the issue.
6	Take the advice of an experienced person.
7	You may be in line for a promotion.
8	A partnership will instinctively evolve and will be successful.
9	You will initially receive small gains until you feel sincere about your actions.
10	Plan any bold moves with caution.
11	Do not force an issue but approach it sensitively and have a clear mind.
12	There are some obstacles that can be averted with firmness and patience.
13	Teamwork will be successful if there is true unity.
14	You will receive great insight and true wisdom.
15	You may have to show humility before succeeding in a big enterprise.
16	Seek a balance and do not reach for easy gratification.
17	There are no obstacles to your plans and you are able to proceed easily.
18	Avoid compulsive behavior and find your inner balance.
19	Although the situation runs smoothly right now, take care of the future.
20	Take the time to contemplate your actions.
21	You may need to engage in some legal action to continue success.
22	You will need to resolve the bigger issue.
23	Do not make any changes yet but examine the past to transform your fears into strengths.

24 Correct a small mistake and continue on your path.

25 Watch out for unexpected events.

26 Help others with your own wealth and wisdom.

27 Look after your health and try to alleviate stress so that your actions are not undermined.

28 Your plan of action is excellent but needs firmer foundations.

29 You must stay in your situation and wait until a way out shows itself.

30 Learn to be tolerant and compliant and you will find your place in the world.

31 Be flexible and open to change.

32 Do not make any changes.

33 Take time to be alone and seek insight from the past about your ambitions.

34 Your plans will be very successful if you are disciplined.

35 Promotion and other material opportunities will follow.

36 Engage in some careful planning and keep your thoughts to yourself.

37 Make a decision after much contemplation and you are guaranteed success.

38 Do not worry about opposition to your plans from others but gain insight from the opposition.

39 Let go of material security to gain new experience.

40 It might be best to retreat from your plan of action.

41 Make sure that you are not overspending or overly exerting yourself.

42 Strengthen your connections before asking for favors.

43 You will face a breakthrough soon if you are resolute in your actions.

44 Try not to get trapped and learn to face your limitations.

45 You will receive rewards and recognition.

46 Continue with your plans.

47 Stay focused on your course of action.

48 Watch out for failure through a mistake.

49 Watch for success when you have achieved inner change.

50 You will have great success.

51 Do not worry about any disturbing news.

52 Keep yourself to yourself, learning the wisdom of silence.

53 You may go ahead with your plans confidently.

54 Do not go ahead with your plans.

55 You will be presented with good opportunities.

56 Try to resolve any conflicts before proceeding on your path.

57 Do not speak your mind until you are ready to act.

58 You will be joyous and successful in your path.

59 You shall attain success by allowing yourself to feel loved and nurtured.

60 It would be advantageous to overcome any relevant limitations.

61 Seek inner information before making a judgment.

62 You are in a dangerous situation; allow the situation to resolve itself and avoid overspending.

63 Watch out for plans that are beginning to look less than favorable.

64 Do not worry if things look unfavorable; they will eventually turn out to your advantage.

NUMEROLOGY

It seems everything has a numerical value. Numbers on a clock face govern us, dictating time, and the dates on a calendar guide us through the year. It is interesting to note that "happy hour" in a bar or club is usually 6 P.M., 6 being a happy number. The "Witching Hour" is midnight, which reduces to 3 (1+2 = 3), a bewitching number. Major events in one's personal life often "coincidentally" happen in threes.

The positive and negative influences that numbers have on our personal destinies are vast and well documented. To practice the art of numerology—predicting the future with numbers—you do not need a good knowledge of mathematics. While this method of fortune-telling is quite simple to practice, it is nonetheless an interesting and powerful way to discover important character traits about yourself and other people, enabling you to better understand them, or them to better understand themselves.

No one's life is so perfect that it would not benefit from the insights numerology can give. Numerology can help guide you in your choice of career path, and can help you learn how to relate better to family and friends. It is also a great advantage to know whose numbers are not compatible with your own.

Many a misunderstood marriage could have been avoided if only the once happy couple had known what to expect from each other. But it is never too late to learn to understand your loved ones. Marriage counselors would be better equipped to help solve the problems of their unhappy clients if they were fully aware of the more subtle causes of conflict.

Employers would be at an advantage when interviewing a prospective employee if they knew how to assess the applicant's compatibility with their requirements. For example, an employer would be able to identify the difference between a dreamer and a genuinely focused achiever.

Numerology includes many methods of revealing the past, present, and future. The following pages show you how to discover your:

- Destiny number
- Birth path number
- Name number
- Personal year number
- Lucky lottery numbers

Another part of numerology, your zodiac number, is discussed under "Astrology" (see pages 62–71). Each of these numbers has a role to play in helping you achieve fulfillment in life.

Once you have mastered these simple techniques, you can use them to entertain your family and friends—they will be amazed.

An important point to remember is that while you generally reduce your personal destiny number, your personal year number, or your name number to a single digit, when you get 11 or 22, do not reduce these to a single digit, because these two numbers have a special power of their own.

Another interesting point to note is that although you cannot change your personal destiny number (because you cannot change the date of your birth) you can change your name number, in order to get maximum benefit from a positive name number, by changing the spelling of your name. Many celebrities have done so, with remarkable results.

Numerology can also help you choose which house you live in. But even if you have no say in this, numerology will help you understand your house number's characteristics. Numerology can give you a better understanding of the people you work with, and if you are running a business, it will show you what destiny number combinations will give you maximum benefits.

Learning the basics of numerology is both fun and useful. You may not be able to control all your important numbers, but self-analysis is so much easier when you know what you are dealing with. You will begin to see where your qualities can best be used, and which shortcomings you need to work on. You will be able to forecast events of the year ahead and the years that follow, which will prepare you for the challenges ahead.

YOUR DESTINY NUMBER

You can quite easily calculate your destiny number by following the procedure demonstrated below.

Write down the date of your birthday. For example, if you were born on February 6, 1970, you write down each number and then simply add all the single digits together: 2+6+1+9+7+0 = 25

Reduce the total: 2+5 = 7

You now know that a person born on this date has a destiny number of 7.

YOUR NAME NUMBER

Numerologists believe the vibrations set off by a particular name can actually affect a behavioral pattern, for better or worse. Many numerologists believe that all names (first, middle, maiden, and married) should be used to calculate your name number, but I would suggest you calculate only those names most often used—these are the ones that are most influential.

1	2	3	4	5	6	7	8	9
A	B	C	D	E	F	G	H	I
J	K	L	M	N	O	P	Q	R
S	T	U	V	W	X	Y	Z	

EXAMPLE:

JONOTHAN   **CITIZEN**

1+6+5+6+1+8+1+5 = 33   +   3+9+2+9+8+5+5 = 41

3+3 = 6   4+1 = 5   6+5 = 11

Better known as **JONO**: 1+6+5+6 = 18; 1+8 = 9

Personality Traits: **6** Sensitive, sensual; **5** Adventurous, argumentative; **11** Independence, leadership; **9** Humanitarian, honorable.

While taking into account the characteristics of these individual numbers, use only the number derived from the name by which you are best known. In this example, Jonothan Citizen = 11, one of the most powerful numbers. Jono Citizen adds up to 5. Because 11 is more powerful than 5, Jonothan would be well advised to forsake "Jono" in favor of his given name.

Refer to the individual meanings of numbers on pages 102–111 to discover the positive and negative influences attached to your destiny and name numbers.

YOUR LUCKY LOTTERY NUMBERS

How many times have you asked yourself: "I wonder which are my lucky numbers?" To find your lucky numbers for the current year, use the number/alphabet graph on the previous page to calculate the numbers of your name. For example:

JIMMY

$1+9+4+4+7 = 25$

$2+5 = 7$

SMITH

$1+4+9+2+8 = 24$

$2+4 = 6$

$6+7 = 13$

$1+3 = 4$

The numbers in bold type (in this example: 25, 24, 7, 6, 13, and 4), plus your destiny number, are your lucky numbers. You will notice that for the purpose of this exercise you are including all the total numbers from your name, plus your destiny number—giving a total of seven numbers. Good luck!

THE MEANINGS OF THE NUMBERS

1 is independent and has organizational and leadership abilities.
Negative traits: tunnel vision, selfishness.

2 is kind and gentle and has an approachable nature.
Negative traits: timid and can be gullible or easily flattered.

3 is versatile, creative, good-natured, and multitalented.
Negative traits: attraction to hedonistic behavior.

4 is practical, stable, dependable, honest, and trustworthy.
Negative traits: stubbornness and an overly serious nature.

5 is extroverted, energetic, resourceful, and daring.
Negative traits: tendency to have too many irons in the fire.

6 is romantic, creative, compassionate, and family oriented.
Negative traits: can be supersensitive and overemotional.

7 is intellectual, philosophical, imaginative, and psychic.
Negative traits: can be impractical, secretive, and unapproachable.

8 is ambitious, tenacious, reliable, honest, and trustworthy.
Negative traits: can be opinionated, impatient, and intolerant.

9 is humanitarian, creative, psychic, sensual, and has healing abilities.
Negative traits: can be self-serving, possessive, and volatile.

11 is concerned with spiritual development, which often leads to an unusual destiny.
Negative traits: can be self-opinionated and vain.

22 is very psychic and has high ideals and goals.
Negative traits: can expect far too much from others and can become tyrannical.

THE POWER OF ONE
RULING PLANET: THE SUN
COLORS: YELLOW, ORANGE, GOLD
GEMSTONES: TOPAZ, AMBER

The power of One attracts pioneering and inventive forces. It signifies originality, independence, and leadership. People with this destiny number tend to stand out in the crowd. They have inventive ideas and want to take over and organize everything—they want to be in charge. Even though they can become unapproachable, other people lean on them for guidance, depending on the One personality to come up with solutions to their problems.

The karmic lessons that a Number One destiny attracts relate to expectations of high achievement, the exploration of new ideas, the reward of success, and the fear of failure. This destiny requires a competitive spirit and a determined, decisive mind. Great physical and mental energy are necessary if Number One characters are to achieve the success they deserve; but "superior beings" are intimidating, so very often people with this number find themselves alone and a little bewildered, because they love being center stage and thrive on applause.

Destiny did not intend Number One personalities to be second best at anything, and they generally choose careers that afford them plenty of scope and control—scientific researchers, politicians, political advisers, inventors, designers, engineers, explorers, and firefighters.

At their best, they shine like their ruling planet, the sun. However, the sun can get in their eyes at times. At their worst, they become so full of self-importance that they begin to believe they can do no wrong. When this happens, they become tyrants who will not suffer fools easily. They are then intolerant and judgmental.
HEALTH: One people are prone to blood pressure, heart disease, and eye problems.

THE TIMID TWO

RULING PLANET: THE MOON
COLORS: GREEN, CREAM
GEMSTONES: PEARL, JADE, MOONSTONE

The timidity of Two comes from the moon's influence on its duality. People whose destiny number is Two prefer to follow and wish to please. They are versatile, sociable, and approachable. They enjoy the art of conversation and are always keen to hear both sides of a story.

The karmic lessons of a Number Two destiny often involve frustration, because these people are afraid of choice. Many Two destinies follow two career paths; they lack a sense of direction and find it difficult to focus. Fate has decreed that they play a support role through life; they don't mind this, because they are too self-conscious to lead.

Number Twos are gentle folk with intuitive and emotional natures. The moon's influence makes Two people insecure, which causes them to seek the company of friends and partners who are dependable and emotionally secure. Mood swings and emotional fragility can cause despair, often resulting in self-pity.

Two people are romantic, sentimental dreamers who require encouragement and reassurance. But Two destiny people are also destined to be the peacemakers of the planet. They are good negotiators, and do well in public relations, sales, and the hospitality industry. They also make good teachers.

Two people make good friends, have a good sense of humor, and are good entertainers. Two children are prone to peer pressure because they like to be popular. An abundance of Twos in a personal numerology chart might indicate some degree of confusion about sexuality.

HEALTH: Two people are subject to digestive and stomach problems. Quite often they suffer from depression.

THE TRI-MENDOUS THREE

RULING PLANET: JUPITER
COLOR: PURPLE, LILAC, MAUVE
GEMSTONE: AMETHYST

This multitalented number attracts creativity, imagination, artistic talents, versatility, and good nature. People with this destiny number are gifted with these blessings.

The karmic lessons of a Three destiny number are designed to teach its owner that hedonistic behavior can be the result of too much luck and too much talent—their highly creative and entrepreneurial personalities will favor the good lifestyle. These highly energized characters are rarely upstaged, because they are competitive as well as gifted.

The entertainment industry brims with Number Three destinies, and it is not difficult to imagine what chaos results from so many egotists in the one place. Luckily they are happy people who do not harbor grudges for long. Even when they are small children, people with a Number Three destiny shine, oozing talent and self-confidence.

As adults they are sociable giants with witty and amusing personalities. Being unpredictable and charming, they make exciting lovers, but also ones who tend to move on when a partner becomes too possessive or boring. Other interesting careers for Three destinies are musician, journalist, and advertising executive.

At their best, Three people will try to use all their skills for the benefit of all. At worst, they spread themselves too thin, which can make them a Jack-of-all-trades and master of none.

Three people can be highly sensitive and can easily develop excessive and addictive behavior patterns. They can be lucky, but they can also be overgenerous and wasteful. "Everything in moderation" should be their motto if they want to evolve spiritually.

HEALTH: Three people are subject to skin problems and other stress-related illnesses.

FOUR SQUARE AND FAIR

RULING PLANET: URANUS
COLORS: BLUE, GRAY
GEMSTONE: SAPPHIRE

The positive qualities of Number Four— practicality, stability, dependability, and good organization—can make people carrying this destiny number the cornerstones of society. They build their lives block by block, but they must be careful not to limit themselves in their efforts to secure a safe environment.

Anyone who crosses the path of a Number Four destiny is richer for the experience, because this hardworking, faithful personality has a steadying influence on everyone. But rarely do Number Fours reap the credit they deserve. Everything these people gain they have earned through dedication to duty and commitment. Born worriers, even in childhood, they take life seriously and suffer headaches and nervous tension early in life.

Four people lack confidence; their greatest need is to be needed. They are always looking for approval but don't often get it— probably because people assume from Four's efficiency that they must already know how valuable they are. As adults they become even more conscientious and dependable, thus making excellent friends, spouses, and parents, but they are overprotective and sometimes possessive, causing their children to leave the nest early. It is small wonder that muscle spasms and neck and head problems seem to plague them in later years.

Four people have a tendency to be too serious, dull, or gloomy, or to worry too excessively. This makes them difficult characters for more extroverted personalities to understand. Four people can be blunt and outspoken, which frightens the more timid Two and Six personalities.

HEALTH: When Four people are not worrying themselves to death, they are reaching for headache medicine or receiving heat treatment for a bad neck ache. Ulcers are common with this number.

FRIVOLOUS FIVE

RULING PLANET: MERCURY
COLORS: GRAY, WHITE
GEMSTONE: DIAMOND

Extroverted, energetic, resourceful, productive, and adventurous are some of the qualities credited to Number Five destinies. They are unpredictable characters, impatient and hungry for the taste of life.

People with this destiny number will try anything at least once, and they'll usually go back for more, even when the adventure is dangerous. The advice people with this number should heed is: "Expect the unexpected" and "Go with the flow," but also "Look before you leap."

Perhaps the reason so many people with Number Five destinies are highly strung is because their karmic lessons involve them in so many varied life experiences. They are mental and physical contortionists. They also become sarcastic and critical under stress and are far too impulsive for their own good, often regretting their behavior.

They are very sociable people and love to talk. They are excitable and exciting to be around, but have more casual than lifelong friends. The media and any other career that requires good communication skills attract Five destinies. They find boredom intolerable because they are active mentally, physically, and spiritually.

Their tendency to be frivolous, argumentative, and changeable, and their moody traits, can cause Five people strife. Because of their low boredom threshold, Number Five destiny children should be kept occupied—they tend to become hyperactive.

Number Five adults can be sexually overactive, because they become bored in the bedroom.

HEALTH: Five people are somewhat accident-prone; they can get hurt swinging from the chandeliers or driving too fast. Insomnia is a common problem for Five people and some suffer from mental disorders.

SENSITIVE SIX
RULING PLANET: VENUS
COLOR: BLUE
GEMSTONE: EMERALD

Typically, because of their ruling planet Venus, people of the Six destiny number are romantic, peace loving, family oriented, compassionate, and considerate creatures who live to love. They are called the "beautiful people," because they are attracted to beautiful things and are born romantics.

The homes of Six destiny people are often filled with arts and crafts of their own creation. They love to potter around, paint, sculpt, and write. Their imagination and creativity give them a flair for interior design. And although they are homebodies at heart, they also need to express their enormous creative talents in a suitable career. Musicians, poets, artists, and interior designers are among the career choices they should make.

More than likely, Six destiny people will choose to work from home. They will never feel lonely, because on the one hand, they tend to be committed to their work, and on the other hand, their home often becomes a magnet for people who seek the nurturing quality of their Six friend. Six destiny people can also work successfully as counselors, particularly with regard to marriage and relationships. They are good listeners and care deeply about their family, friends, and clients.

The spouse and children of a Six parent are blessed, because it is within the family environment that Sixes excel. However, when they have an excess of these qualities, they become overly protective of their loved ones. They become perfectionists, which can be difficult, as we all live on an imperfect planet, and because of this they tend to resent constructive criticism. Six people should guard against vanity.

HEALTH: Six people tend to suffer from poor circulation and heart disease. The throat and kidney areas are also weak spots for many Six people.

SOLITARY SEVEN

RULING PLANET: NEPTUNE
COLOR: GREEN
GEMSTONE: MOONSTONE

Positive traits of the Seven personal destiny number are that they are intellectual, philosophical, imaginative, solitary, and psychically gifted. They are attracted to the ocean's vibration and its green/blue colors, and they like to live near water. Seven people are very private, but they are not necessarily unapproachable. They are attracted to all things mythical and mystical.

This is a very intense personality, constantly searching for the meaning of life and the hereafter. They are intensely sensitive to vibration, which is why they must have a tranquil environment in which to live and work; they are in tune with nature and abhor imitations. They are very psychic beings, and the solitude they seek intensifies this ability.

Sevens love to explore the religious and spiritual beliefs of foreign cultures, and making a pilgrimage to remote parts of the world is not an uncommon practice with them. Having gathered this knowledge, they prefer to lock their souls away in a quest for privacy and reflection.

Career paths that involve a degree of contemplation would suit most Seven people. They are often found in scientific research, libraries, and bookstores; they also make good writers and music composers.

Negative traits of this number are impracticality, secretiveness, unapproachability, moodiness, and laziness. Also, Seven people can be very unrealistic. They live in a world of their own and must be careful not to cut themselves off from the rest of society too often.

Children with this destiny number should be encouraged to share their gifts with the rest of the world.

HEALTH: Seven people may suffer from nervous disorders and depression. They often have problems with their "waterworks," their kidneys, and related organs.

EXTREMIST EIGHT

RULING PLANET: SATURN
COLOR: BLACK, PURPLE
GEMSTONES: RUBY, AMETHYST

People with this personal destiny number have ambition, drive, tenacity, and an appreciation of material things. Eight people admire those who are strong-willed and strong-minded. They are outspoken and opinionated, but very loyal.

Eight people have feast-or-famine destinies and all-or-nothing attitudes. They were born "old souls," which makes them appear to know it all—even in childhood. The old adage "When they're good they're very, very good and when they're bad they're horrid" fits Eight people. They are people of substance and born organizers. A good environment is essential to them.

Eight people rarely try anything until they have made sure they can be good at it. Career paths Eight people generally enjoy include corporate business, the law, banking, and accountancy.

Eight people are often less than enthusiastic about the feast-or-famine destiny fate has dealt them; they need to remember that they have as many positive experiences as negative ones. They cannot see the logic of a higher intelligence, which allows them to work hard toward their goals, shows them the reward of their efforts, and then pulls the rug out from under them. Their inner strength seems to be constantly tested, often causing them to wonder how much more they have to do in order to receive their just reward.

It is difficult for them to understand their karmic lessons, because the lessons are not tangible. Once they accept their seesaw existence, they usually find a way to deal with it by storing up the positive benefits for a rainy day.

Eight people may have a tendency toward arrogance, obstinacy, extremism, and ruthlessness; they may also suffer from depression.
HEALTH: Eight people may suffer skin problems, troubles with their teeth, and rheumatic complaints.

NOTORIOUS NINE
RULING PLANET: MARS
COLOR: RED
GEMSTONE: BLOODSTONE

People with the Nine destiny number are humanitarian creatures who wish to save the world. Like Eights, they are very old souls; they are also psychic. They "see red" when injustice is done. They are sensual people, easily attracting the opposite sex, with whom they love to flirt, being naturally hot-blooded.

The karmic lessons of a Nine destiny involve the well-being of humanity. Nines are often missionaries and visionaries, and flock to underdeveloped countries to fight for the spiritual and physical growth of humankind. They want to save the planet and its occupants from self-destruction, and sometimes become martyrs to this cause.

The influence of the fighting spirit of the planet Mars on Nine people inspires them to pursue these goals with grit and guts. They are intrigued by the paranormal because they have great insight and innate psychic powers. They crave affection and are passionate lovers. Their supersensitive natures are easily offended, and they do not forgive easily.

Careers that attract Nine people are the medical field, welfare, religious orders, veterinary science, animal welfare, parks and wildlife, environmental organizations, and the visual arts. Circus people often have multiple Nines in their numerology charts.

Nine personalities may have a tendency toward possessiveness, neurosis, and volatility. God help the person they are fatally attracted to, because they won't let this person out of their sight for long. Promiscuity can be a problem for them because they are constantly being pursued and they love flattery.

HEALTH: Nine people may suffer problems around the genitals and kidney areas.

ELEVATED ELEVEN AND TREMENDOUS TWENTY-TWO

Most numerologists attach a great deal of importance to the power of 11 and 22, preferring not to reduce them to Two or Four.

Even when numerologists reduce 11 and 22 when calculating a numerology chart, they will usually take the power of each into consideration, because often both 11 and 22 belong to people whose destinies are important and unusual. They have strong psychic ability and appear to be highly evolved spiritually.

Two examples of famous names are:

JESUS: 1+5+1+3+1 = 11

ELVIS: 5+3+4+9+1 = 22

Both brought powerful, lasting influences to the planet, albeit for very different reasons. Both were relatively short-lived and both lives ended tragically.

In some ways these two numbers, 11 and 22, are contradictory. The personality with an Eleven destiny number has a karma of independence and leadership as well as the karma of the reduced number 1+1 = 2—that of a dependent follower—to cope with.

Interestingly, Jesus was a powerful leader who attracted many followers. Elvis depended on his followers to achieve his fame, which he guarded with elaborate security measures—the result of the security conscious Four (2+2) destiny number.

One is the number of revelation and spiritual insight. The eleventh card of the tarot's Major Arcana is "Justice." When someone has completed their search for truth and insight it will be revealed by the appearance of this card in their layout. The number 22 is the number of completion and perfection. The final card of the Major Arcana is Number 22, "The World," the symbol of completion.

YOUR PERSONAL YEAR NUMBER

Apart from the importance of your destiny number and your name number, each new year has a number of its own—1998: 1+9+9+8 = 27 = 9, for example. Hence the number 9, whose qualities include humanitarianism, spirituality, and psychic evolvement, governed the year of 1998—it is no coincidence that psychic awareness is becoming increasingly popular. To calculate your personal year number, follow these instructions:

If your birthday is February 1, 1934, and the present year is 2003, you would replace 1934 with 2003: 2+1+2+0+0+3 = 8; so your personal year number for 2003 would be 8.

If your birthday is March 15, 1972, change 1972 to 2003. This will then give you 3+1+5+2+0+0+3 = 14; 1+4 = 5, so 5 is your personal year number for 2003.

Refer to the individual meanings of the numbers on pages 102–111 to discover the positive and negative influences affecting you for this year.

Refer to the opposite page for the prevailing influences of each year.

YOUR LUCKY YEAR NUMBER

As everyone knows, some years are luckier and happier than others. A year when the value of positive and compatible numbers is evident is considered a lucky year in numerology. So, which are your personal lucky years?

In numerology, the world turns in nine-year cycles, and every nine years your destiny number is the same as the current year number—these years are believed to be your luckiest years. However, there is more than one lucky year in each cycle. When your destiny number, zodiac number (see pages 63–71), and personal year number are all the same, then you are in a year of extremes—it will be truly a "feast or famine" period.

PERSONAL YEAR NUMBERS AND THEIR INFLUENCES

1 In this beginning of a new nine-year cycle fate gives you a clean sheet of paper and says, "Write your own script." You are in control of the events in your life and should make the most of new beginnings and fresh adventures.

2 Peace, harmony, balance, communication. This is a year in which you want to develop personal relationships; many people marry or make commitments in this year.

3 Your creative skills should be used to their full potential in this year. It is a fruitful, fertile year and it is lucky, because of Jupiter's influence. This is a good year to start a family.

4 Concentrate on building up your resources and your personal and family security. This year is also favorable for focusing on study and working hard toward a goal.

5 Expect the unexpected in terms of travel, change, challenge, and new experiences. It's a year of adventure, but flow with the tide, because a Five Year is like a kaleidoscope, forever changing patterns. You need to be energized, alert, and ready for the challenges this year will bring.

6 Fate demands that you take care of the family in a Six Year. Family matters should be settled, and the beauty of family life appreciated. This is a year of romance.

7 This is a year of introspection: you should take this opportunity to examine your inner being and bring intellectual pursuits to fruition.

8 This year attracts conditions that can bring either financial benefits or financial losses—or both! It's a time when you feel strongly about your finances; one moment you're saving every cent and the next you're going on a spending spree. People in an Eight Year often seem moody and changeable.

9 This is your emotional spring-cleaning year. Bring all your emotional experiences out into the open, keeping only those things of proven value. Add only positive emotional experiences. Any emotional excess baggage you might have been carrying during the previous eight years must be dealt with and abandoned in preparation for the beginning of a new One Year.

DOES YOUR DESTINY NUMBER COMPLEMENT YOUR HOUSE NUMBER?

Some numerologists believe in using the Fadic system to calculate the house number value, and others believe that all the numbers of the house should be taken into consideration. The Fadic system is the simple method of reducing numbers: apartment 20 at number 231 Smith Street would be 20/231 Smith Street = 2+0+2+3+1 = 8. Only the value of 8 is taken into consideration.

Numerologists who believe in assessing the value of all these numbers would take the importance of a double 2, and the 3 and 1 into consideration. A house number 44, with more than one Four personality living there, would most likely have bars on the window and a top security alarm system—4 is a security-conscious number that creates nervous tension. A house with too many 5s (an

extroverted and liberated number) can quickly gain a reputation for being too loud.

The following pages serve as a guide to the characteristics attributed to your house number.

House Number One

POSITIVE TRAITS: Creates good energy and positive vibrations

NEGATIVE TRAITS: Evokes selfishness and snobbery in negative tenants

BEST COMPANIONS: Destiny numbers 1, 3, 8

SUMMATION: This is a trendsetters' dream house, which calls out to be occupied by a pioneering spirit who dares to take advantage of its inventive energy. This house likes plenty of sunlight and fresh air and its positive vibrations are enhanced by the colors yellow, gold, and orange. A Number 1 house requires a good fire alarm system because it is subject to fire hazards.

House Number Two

POSITIVE TRAITS: Creates peace, harmony, and balance

NEGATIVE TRAITS: Evokes laziness and insecurity in negative tenants

BEST COMPANIONS: Destiny numbers 2, 6, 9

SUMMATION: Not a good choice for the ambitious, career-minded spirit. This house is far better suited to laid-back, friendly people. Young lovers and longtime partners suit this house because its loving vibration prefers couples to single or multiple owners. A cream, green, or white decor enhances its harmonious vibration.

House Number Three

POSITIVE TRAITS: Creates a happy, sociable vibration

NEGATIVE TRAITS: Evokes extravagance and noisiness in negative tenants

BEST COMPANIONS: Destiny numbers 1, 3, 5

SUMMATION: This house has creative energy and is very welcoming. Music lovers, actors, and entrepreneurs beat a path to the door. It is a lucky house, often of unusual design. Mauve and lilac will have a calming effect on noisy, restless tenants. Owners of a Number 3 house often overinvest, making the house feel cluttered.

House Number Four

POSITIVE TRAITS: Creates an orderly existence and a secure vibration

NEGATIVE TRAITS: Has an unlived-in appearance when occupied by negative tenants

BEST COMPANIONS: Destiny numbers 4, 7, 8

SUMMATION: This house welcomes neat, orderly occupants who will keep it in good repair. Blue, gray, and muted colors are favorites, and being an earthy house, it likes lots of indoor plants. Structural problems are sometimes a headache for the owners. Bars on the windows and locks on the doors will be the general impression this house gives when occupied by negative tenants.

House Number Five

POSITIVE TRAITS: Creates challenges and an uninhibited vibration

NEGATIVE TRAITS: Evokes arguments and tempers in negative tenants

BEST COMPANIONS: Destiny numbers 1, 3, 5

SUMMATION: A Number 5 house often becomes labeled "a temporary dwelling" because the vibration is one of change, challenge, and new experience, thus encouraging its tenants to move on or to be frequently away from home, leaving the premises subject to theft. Variety is the key word, so the owner often has different ideas for every room.

House Number Six

POSITIVE TRAITS: Creates a peaceful, loving, tranquil vibration

NEGATIVE TRAITS: Evokes interference from negative neighbors

BEST COMPANIONS: Destiny numbers 2, 3, 4, 6, 9

SUMMATION: A Number 6 house evokes considerate, romantic, creative, and homey instincts from its tenants. Music enhances these positive traits, and even negative tenants benefit from the harmonious forces in a Number 6 house.

House Number Seven

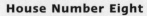

POSITIVE TRAITS: Creates a serene and mystical vibration

NEGATIVE TRAITS: Evokes secretiveness and loneliness in negative tenants

BEST COMPANIONS: Destiny numbers 7, 9

SUMMATION: The vibration of a Number 7 house attracts mystical, intellectual, philosophical, imaginative people, as well as seekers of solitude. This house encourages its occupants to develop their spiritual and psychic abilities. Wishing wells, ponds, fountains, and pools enhance its serenity. Orchids and four-leaf clovers love this dwelling, but the energy of this house number can evoke loneliness and secretiveness in negative tenants. Problems with the plumbing system often arise in a Number 7 house.

House Number Eight

POSITIVE TRAITS: Creates ambition and material benefits

NEGATIVE TRAITS: Evokes extreme behavioral patterns in negative tenants

BEST COMPANIONS: Destiny numbers 1, 4, 8

SUMMATION: A Number 8 house complements the hardworking, ambitious qualities of positive tenants. People best suited to a Number 8 house are focused types. It is a solid house whose owners keep it that way. Moss green and cream, blues, and grays all suit the Number 8 house. Trees, plants, and flowers native to the area enhance this dwelling. Negative tenants may experience extreme behavioral problems, and their negative character traits may be exacerbated.

House Number Nine

POSITIVE TRAITS: Creates humanitarian vocational instincts in its occupants

NEGATIVE TRAITS: Evokes self-righteous, sanctimonious behavior in negative tenants

BEST COMPANIONS: Destiny numbers 2, 6, 9

SUMMATION: A Number 9 house inspires mental and spiritual growth and as such will attract medical people, visionaries, and welfare workers. People who create an atmosphere of belonging are welcome. Its garden loves daffodils, roses, and carnations. Psychic awareness may be evoked in its occupants. It is, however, an accident-prone environment for negative tenants.

A SAMPLE NUMEROLOGICAL PROFILE FOR "JOHN BLACK"

DESTINY NUMBER, BASED ON DATE OF BIRTH 10-3-1963

$1+0+3+1+9+6+3 = 23; 2+3 = 5$

NAME NUMBER

JOHN   BLACK

$1+6+8+5$ + $2+3+1+3+2 = 31$ $3+1 = 4$

LUCKY NUMBERS (BASED ON NAME)

$1+6+8+5$ + $2+3+1+3+2$

20   **11**

$2+0 = 2$ $1+1 = 2$

NUMEROLOGICAL PROFILE

Destiny Number: 5 • *Name Number:* 4

Health: Insomnia, nervous disorders, overactive thyroid, respiratory problems

Lucky Colors: Gray and other light colors

Lucky Gemstones: Diamonds

Lucky Lottery Numbers: 2, 4, 5, 11, 20, 31

Best Companions: Destiny numbers 1, 3, 8

Lucky Years: 1967, 1976, 1985, 1994, 2003, 2012, 2021, 2030, 2039, 2048

PERSONALITY PROFILE

Travel, change, challenge, and new experiences are the key words for John's destiny. Fate has dealt him a wide variety of karmic lessons through which to fulfill his commitment to life. He no doubt views his life as though it is something he sees looking through a kaleidoscope—blink your eye and the pattern has changed. As if to make things more interesting—or annoying—John's inclination will be to find solitude. Fate will often deny him the privacy he craves to explore his extremely intelligent, creative, philosophical mind.

His wish to pay serious attention to his scholarly and creative studies will often be distracted by fate's intervention, when his destiny decrees he should be involved—albeit temporarily—in more earthly pursuits.

As a child, John would have been inclined to hang back, not wishing to enjoy the limelight at school—a wasted effort, because his teachers would not have failed to see the intellectual talent of this student. As an adult, he is likely to be following his innate desire to travel to remote places where he can further develop his creative/philosophical skills. His reputation for being a focused and loyal worker (name number 4) will mean he is well regarded by his employers and appreciated by his spouse and children.

P

PALMISTRY

Palmistry has been a favorite method of fortune-telling ever since the time of the ancient Hindus, who are credited with its origin.

The lines, mounts, and other markings found on the palms of the hands seem to tell a story. It is about our journey on life's highways and byways, gathering experience as we go. If you take the time to study the unique map etched out on the palms of your hands, you will discover not only the quality and length of your personal journey, but also advantageous routes and warning signs signaling the danger spots.

Well-defined lines that are long and uninterrupted signify positive qualities connected with that line; broken, weak lines indicate setbacks and disadvantages.

The Main Lines in your hand—the Life Line, Heart Line, and Head Line—are like the main highways. The Minor Lines—the Affection or Marriage Lines, Fate Line, Health Line, Travel Lines, and Girdle of Venus, among others—are similar to other roadways

and paths: they are accessible to those who wish to travel them. The thumb is like a set of road signs indicating which route you are likely to follow. The fingers are also similar to traffic signs: they signal your ability or inability to cope with your predestined journey.

Well-developed mounts (see illustration on page 139) signify positive energy that comes from the planetary influences governing the mounts. The mounts of Jupiter, Saturn, Apollo, Mercury, Venus, Neptune, Mars, and the Moon are not unlike well-used, reliable, and favorable routes. The absence of any or all of these mounts seems to indicate a lack of opportunity to use these particular services.

Markings on the palm of the hand, such as crosses, stars, forks, grids, chains, islands, and dots, are all significant signs of good or bad fortune. They may be warning you to "proceed with caution" or signifying a safe and enjoyable crossing. Either way, these markings should be carefully studied (see illustration on page 133).

Misreading the signs can lead to misconceptions, causing alarm and distress where it may not be necessary. One of the most common misconceptions in palmistry is caused by a short Life Line. It may seem a natural assumption, because of the nature of this line's name, that if it appears to suddenly end at an early age, then so too does your life end.

Think about it logically: if this were true, all the Main Lines would have to end at the same early age, plus there would have to be some significant markings on these lines, also at the same early age, indicating misfortune. After all, you can't have a heart, a head, and a destiny without a life. A good palmist will look for far more detail than a short Life Line before declaring a short life span. If you are a student of palmistry, this is an important lesson to remember.

Reading the palms of your hands is a fascinating study of life. At its best, it is an accurate account of your past, present, and future life. The more you look, the more you see. The more attention you give to the detailed warning signs, the less trouble you will have. If you take notice of the positive signs, you are less likely to miss chances for successful ventures and personal happiness.

Palmistry has been fascinating people all over the world for many years. You will be amazed at your popularity when you can take the hand of a friend or stranger and surprise them with your observations and predictions. Try to combine your newfound skills with your intuition in order to develop the psychic ability that is available to all of us.

THE SHAPE OF YOUR HANDS

There are several shapes and textures of hands to be considered, and they can show at a glance some of the characteristics of the person. The shapes of the hands, fingers, and thumb are important indicators of attitude and degree of dedication to the journey through life. From the shape of the hand alone you can tell whether the person is driven by logic or sentiment, whether they are pedantic or lackadaisical, whether they are creative or practical. Defining the shape of a hand is not difficult if you know what to look for and get into the habit of observing the hands of the people you meet every day. And the "language" of the hands—the handshake, sweaty palms, demonstrative hands—also indicates behavioral patterns.

Both hands must be taken into account in palmistry. The major hand, which is the one you write with, can appear to be, and often is, very different from the minor hand. The simple explanation of these differences is that the minor hand will show the potential you are born with, and the major hand will show if and when you reach this potential. For instance, many gifted qualities shown on the minor hand are absent or faint on the major hand. This means these talents have been unrealized, for whatever reason. Lack of opportunity, illness, or disorganization can temporarily stop the flow of energy that inspires us to fulfill our potential.

The "river" of life can be calm and inspiring or turbulent and destructive. The "highway" of life can be barren or fruitful. Life is a journey and palmistry can be your personal guide, mapping out the way you choose to travel.

The square hand

A square hand is so called when the base of the fingers and the ends of the fingers are equal in width. These are the hands of people who are down-to-earth, industrious, and honest. What you see is what you get with these folks. They have a realistic approach to life. They are sensible and resourceful types who are well equipped to travel the highway of life, preferring to stick to the proven roadways, infrequently using detours.

Square-handed people are attracted to careers that require hard work and good business sense. It is uncommon to find weak, fragmented lines on the square hand. Well-defined, unblemished lines are far more common.

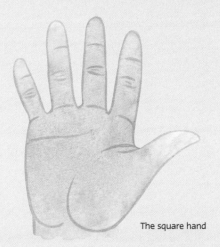

The square hand

Unlike the other hand shapes, the position and the shape of the thumb is important on a square hand. To determine the positioning of the thumb, press the thumb against the Jupiter (index) finger and see how high up the top of the thumb reaches. When the thumb is well positioned—when the top comes halfway up the bottom phalange (lowest of the three sections) of the Jupiter finger and is straight—the qualities of the square hand are enhanced.

A thumb that reaches any point below this level is considered short. This means the normally principled square-handed person allows the influence of others to weaken his or her willpower. When a short thumb also has a bulbous or clubbed shape it is labeled the "elementary hand"; this indicates a passionate nature that sometimes lacks control. Intellectually disabled people usually have a "short clubbed" thumb.

When the thumb is long—extending into the second (middle) phalange of the Jupiter finger—the person will combine their practical industrious qualities with strong leadership abilities.

A flexible, flat thumb, leaning backward, is rarely found on a square hand.

See more about thumbs on pages 126–127.

The clubbed thumb   The flexible or flat thumb

The spatulate hand

The spatula-shaped hand is wide at the fingertips and narrow at the base of the hand, the wrist. It is the hand of the adventurous spirit, the explorer who loves challenge and new experiences. People with this hand shape are daring and confrontational. Rarely will they tolerate a boring journey through life. They look for adventure around every corner; for them, "variety is the spice of life." They have investigative minds and are energetic and motivated.

The conic hand

The conic hand is sometimes called the feminine hand, because it is gently rounded, and because people with this hand shape generally have sensitive, creative natures. They love creature comforts and are optimistic. They are peace loving, family oriented, and approachable. They are caring people who prefer to journey through life with a special partner. Delicate curving lines and a well-developed Mount of Venus are common to this hand; a Head Line curving down toward the Mount of the Moon is indicative of creative abilities.

The knotted hand

These "intellectual" hands belong to the philosophical personality. Alert, creative, and aware of their karmic journey, these people at times become pedantic about the details of their observations. They are interesting and inquisitive mental travelers who make good companions and teachers. Never tired of learning, people with knotted hands absorb knowledge like a sponge. They prefer to live and work in a tranquil environment where they can escape into the realms of creativity and new ideas.

The spatulate hand   The conic hand   The knotted hand

The pointed hand

This hand shape is also known as the "psychic" hand—the fingers are delicate, long, and tapered, indicating sensitivity and imagination. People with pointed hands find it difficult to hide their feelings. They have sympathetic, compassionate natures, and their need for plenty of affection causes them to fall in love easily. They go through life with a refined and reserved attitude. Disliking confrontation, they often hide their true feelings. They are creatively gifted, with a high degree of ESP, and need to be appreciated.

The mixed hand

The mixed hand may seem like an oddity and is hard to define. It is indicative of an interesting personality who views every stage in the journey of life from a different perspective.

The mixed hand is a mixture of two or more of the types previously identified, and all the personality traits attributed to these types should be taken into account. For instance, a more developed radial side (thumb side) of the hand signifies a personality with a strong interest in material or worldly affairs, whereas a hand that is more developed on the ulnar (little finger) side is suggestive of a character more interested in the creative, imaginative side of life.

Long fingers on a square palm indicate creative, artistic qualities governed by a practical mind. A square palm with short, round fingers is indicative of a quick-witted, fast-acting personality.

Special attention should be paid to the size, shape, and flexibility of the thumb on a mixed hand, because this will add to or detract from the qualities found in the rest of the hand. People with this hand seem to go through life with varying degrees of interest in their karmic path, usually with interesting results.

The pointed hand   The mixed hand with short   The mixed hand with longer
fingers and a square palm   fingers and a square palm

YOUR FINGERS

Your fingers tell you how to use your talents and energies to their best advantage. For instance, long-fingered people are not self-motivated, but they are talented and patient. Short-fingered people have initiative and are self-motivated, but they dislike repetitive work.

The setting of the fingers on the palm of the hand varies. Fingers set in a straight line indicate an ambitious personality. A gentle curve in the formation signifies a balanced personality, and a V-shaped setting indicates an insecure nature.

Each finger is divided into three sections, called phalanges. The top phalange represents thought, the middle phalange represents will, and the bottom phalange represents action. Shapes of fingers show some other personality traits:

A Thick, short fingers are indicative of an impatient, rash nature. People with these fingers are focused and honest but display little tact and do not care for trivial pursuits.

B Thin fingers belong to precise people with logical minds and diplomatic natures.

C Knobby knuckles indicate a cautious, sometimes pedantic nature, especially if the top knuckles are knobbed.

D If the middle knuckle is knotted, it signifies a personality with an orderly mind and just the right degree of logic.

Each finger is linked to the energy of a celestial body—Jupiter, Saturn, Apollo, and Mercury.

The Jupiter finger

The Jupiter, or index, finger relates to originality in religion, politics, and leadership. A long Jupiter finger represents a personality that is independent and strong-willed, with deeply spiritual, religious, philosophical beliefs. These people have great leadership ability and like control, often seeking power and material gain.

A short Jupiter finger indicates a person who lacks confidence. Constructive criticism tends to make these people feel inadequate. Being of a caring nature, they are open to manipulation—they need to learn to have more confidence in their own judgment.

The Saturn finger

The Saturn, or second, finger is serious and down-to-earth. It represents the logical, practical, materialistic things in life. The person with a long Saturn finger is serious, with a great ability to concentrate and absorb study.

A short Saturn finger means the person is prepared to take on challenges in business ventures, but if the Apollo finger is long and leans toward the Saturn finger then the challenges become risks, and the person will often lean toward gambling. Famous show-business personalities tend to have the Saturn, Apollo, and Jupiter fingers more or less of the same length. If the Saturn finger is only moderately short, it denotes an ability to win using intuition; but people with short Saturn fingers tend to let their winnings slip through their fingers.

The Apollo finger

The Apollo, or third, finger represents the sun—growth, expansion, luck, fame, and fortune. A long Apollo finger is indicative of a family-oriented nature, someone who likes peace and harmony. Someone with a long Apollo finger is willing, approachable, energetic, sociable, and creative. He or she is a romantic who loves music, the arts, and anything that adds beauty to life.

A short Apollo finger indicates a nature that is self-motivated and sometimes selfish. It also signifies an insecure personality—someone who is constantly seeking reassurance.

The Mercury finger

The Mercury, or little (pinky), finger represents the skills needed for communication, medicine, literature, teaching, and humanitarian activities. A long Mercury finger increases the communication skills bestowed by the Mercury influence on this finger. It also indicates curiosity in the mind of its possessor. Journalistic and creative skills are also attributed to the long Mercury finger. These personalities attract other intellectual and interesting minds and capture the imagination of an audience with their talent for public speaking and teaching. They are good negotiators and organizers.

A short Mercury finger indicates shyness and a reserved nature, lacking in confidence. In contrast to the long Mercury finger, the short version is introverted and dislikes public speaking.

YOUR THUMB AND NAILS

Even at a glance, the thumb is a strong indicator of personality type and business acumen. The thumbnail showing side-on when the hand is relaxed (palm up) indicates someone who is in control of their actions but is nevertheless easygoing. The thumbnail sitting at the back of the hand (with the hand still palm up) shows a self-disciplined person who is both consistent and persistent but who also has tunnel vision or is narrow-minded. To determine the length of the thumb—long, normal, or short—refer to page 121.

The nail section or first phalange of the thumb shows the person's degree of willpower. A long first phalange demonstrates a strong-willed, intelligent mind. A short phalange indicates a person who is likely to use their physical energy in conjunction with their mental energy and willpower, such as in athletic endeavors. A square top to the first phalange represents a practical and sensible nature with a desire to lead.

The shape of the nails can also provide information about medical conditions and personality. For instance:

- Short, square nails are indicative of a quick-witted, quick-tempered, argumentative, critical, and jealous person whose energy levels are generally high.
- Long nails are indicative of a cautious, reliable, and affectionate personality with fairly low energy levels.
- Round nails indicate a good-natured, kind, placid, sensitive, and sensible person with a good energy flow.
- Spatulate (spatula-shaped) nails indicate a temperamental, moody, ambitious, and competitive person who tends to be prone to long-term illness.
- Narrow nails indicate an ambitious, materialistic, and headstrong personality who tends to suffer from delicate lungs.

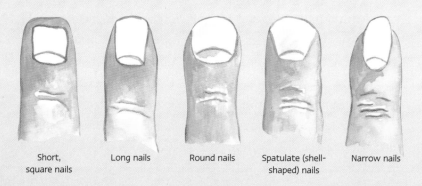

| Short, square nails | Long nails | Round nails | Spatulate (shell-shaped) nails | Narrow nails |

A high-set thumb has an angle of about 45 degrees. It indicates an overly cautious and emotionally restrictive personality who is a creature of habit. A low-set thumb has an angle of about 90 degrees; this is indicative of an extroverted, adventurous, enthusiastic temperament. Many famous people have a thumb that is low set.

A square-top thumb belongs to a dependable personality who is well organized and hardworking—what you see is what you get.

A conic top represents a personality with an easygoing nature. These people are kind, gentle folk who are sometimes easily influenced.

A spatulate top, sometimes nicknamed the "worker's thumb," has acquired this label because this personality has a preference for manual crafts, putting creative skills to practical use.

A round top is indicative of a well-rounded personality; this person can balance her own will with authority and is able to respect the will of others.

A flat top means refinement but a lack of energy—some people with this shape develop skills of manipulation through their charm and powers of persuasion.

A pointed top shows a person who needs to be loved and appreciated. At times these people become too eager in their desire for approval; this makes them easy targets for controlling predators.

BRACELETS

"Rascettes" or "bracelets" are names given to the two or three lines that run across the wrist. Many Eastern palmists used the number of bracelets to determine the length of the subject's life. The practice was to attribute thirty years of life to each bracelet: two full-width bracelets and one half bracelet would therefore predict a life span of seventy-five years, and three full-width bracelets would mean a span of ninety years. Modern palmists debate this belief. However, it is agreed that well-defined and long bracelets are indicative of a fortunate and healthy life, while short and delicate-looking bracelets suggest a more difficult and less energetic life.

YOUR LINES

Discovering the quality and length of your journey through life, plus knowing whether you are traveling on or off the beaten track, is valuable information, and it can be gained by studying the lines on the palm of your hand.

The Life, Head, and Heart Lines are the most easily identifiable and are known as the Main Lines. The Fate Line is also considered by many palmists to be a Main Line, but it doesn't appear on everyone's hand. However, it is a complex line and deserves treatment equal to that of the other Main Lines.

Less identifiable are the Apollo, Simian, Marriage and Children Lines, the Health Line, the Girdle of Venus, the Line of Intuition and the Medical Line—these are known as the Minor Lines (see pages 134–137).

You will be amazed at how quickly you become familiar with the positions of the Major and Minor Lines, and how easy it then becomes to interpret the meanings of the signs that appear on them (see page 133).

It is important to remember that just as the forces of nature can cause turbulence and then restore tranquility, so too the mind and body are equipped to deal with the forces operating within and outside the body. The hand—which is, after all, a living organ—displays signs of trauma and good fortune, past, present, and future.

By observing the warning signs nature provides for you in the palms of your hands, traumatic disturbances may be avoided—your palm will later show a more peaceful, healthy, and rewarding experience. And by taking note of your special talents, as displayed on your palm, you can explore their development to expand and enrich your life's journey.

The Life Line

The Life Line begins its journey about halfway between the base (outside edge) of the Jupiter (index) finger and the base of the thumb. It travels out and downward toward the wrist, encircling the ball of the thumb. If life were perfect, you would discover a long, unbroken, well-defined line free of markings. However, if the Life Line is faint and does not have a double or sister line to support it, this heralds weakness, such as a poor energy level or even a poor quality of life.

The formative years—birth to teens—extend from the beginning

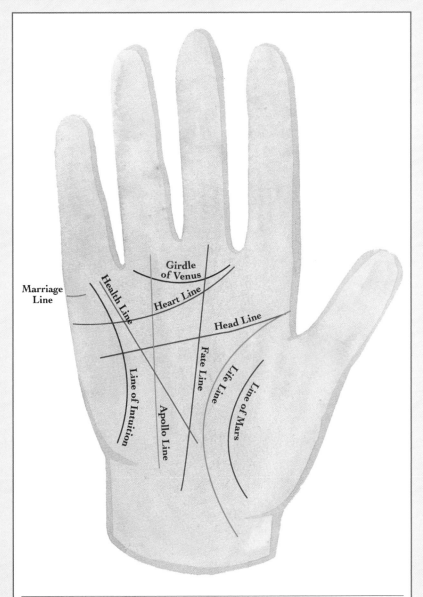

HEALTH LINE: this line will appear when there is a health problem and disappear once health is restored.

MARRIAGE LINE: number and depth of serious relationships.

HEART LINE: emotions, sensuality, and the health of the heart.

APOLLO LINE: home, family, creativity, the arts and fortune.

LINE OF INTUITION: represents intuition and psychic ability.

LINE OF MARS: adds extra energy to the Life Line.

LIFE LINE: life force, energy, drive. This represents the way we choose to travel through life and our physical health.

HEAD LINE: the intellect, the mind, career, and mental health.

FATE LINE: the way we work, our partnerships, and success or failure.

GIRDLE OF VENUS: represents sensuality and sexuality.

of the Life Line to a point directly beneath the center of the Jupiter finger. In this section of the Life Line, you will often find the Life Line attached to the Head Line, so that they appear to be one line. This represents the interaction between the mind of the child and the influence of the parent or guardian. Often this line has a chained effect—this usually signifies some physical or emotional difficulties during childhood.

A Life Line that appears to cling closely to the thumb is indicative of a person who prefers to stay in the familiar environment of their homeland. It also signifies caution, sensitivity, and a lack of energy and drive. A Life Line that swoops out, encircling the Mount of Venus, is usually associated with a person who embraces the energy and adventure of life. A line or lines that cross from the Life Line into the Mount of the Moon indicate that a person will enjoy the thrill of travel.

A line drooping down from the inside of the Life Line usually indicates a loss, such as a divorce or death in the family, that is a traumatic experience. Islands, breaks, dots, and crosses on the Life Line indicate temporary setbacks to the natural flow of the life force (see also page 133).

The Head Line

The Head Line (see illustration on page 129) begins its journey at or about the same point as the Life Line. It travels across the palm toward the outer edge. A Head Line that is well developed, long, and straight indicates a practical mind and success in business—it is a sign of the clear, level-minded thinking of a hardworking person. A short but well-defined line denotes great powers of concentration and determined ambition. A faint or fragile-looking line, whether it is short or long, tends to be associated with a mind that is easily distracted and becomes bored with long periods of study.

A Head Line that slopes down deep inside the Mount of the Moon suggests a supersensitive nature, moodiness, fears, and phobic behavior, which can lead to depression. When this line tilts upward at the end it means success in business.

Branches turning upward at intervals on the Head Line are indicative of concentrated bursts of mental effort at the time they appear. Branches swooping downward from the Head Line show periods of mental fatigue and stress. A fork at the end of a long Head Line is associated with a longer than average working life filled with many outside interests. If the Head Line has a "tasseled" appearance, it is a sign of worry.

A double Head Line requires special attention, because it is indicative of a multitalented person who is capable of achieving success in more than one career, but who has little time for personal relationships. This person will therefore be a difficult personality to relate to or hold on to, likely to pursue a career that demands practical business acumen at the same time as he or she is pursuing a career as a professional artist, performer, or athlete.

Islands, breaks, dots, and crosses on the Head Line will appear during times of misfortune, such as setbacks, illnesses, or accidents (see page 133).

The Heart Line

The Heart Line (see illustration on page 129), whether it is curved or straight, begins from a point somewhere between the Jupiter (index) finger and the Saturn (second) finger, and travels across the palm to a point beneath the Mercury (little) finger. It represents the emotional side of a person's nature as well as giving information about certain areas of health.

Health information about the heart and lungs is stored in the section of the Heart Line below the base of the Mercury finger. A Heart Line that begins under the Jupiter finger suggests a sensuous and spiritual nature, and a person who makes a lot of demands on his or her partner. A Heart Line that starts beneath the Saturn finger indicates a person who is sentimental, affectionate, and placid. These people need romance to stir their sensuous, passionate side.

A straight Heart Line is often associated with a person who is emotionally controlled, especially if the Head Line is more clearly defined than the Heart Line. The more curved the Heart Line appears to be, the more emotional and sensual the person is. People with curved lines are not afraid to openly show their emotions; nor are they afraid to express their disappointments in love.

If there are branches leading downward from the Heart Line, the person is cautious in forming relationships for fear of rejection, probably due to a past traumatic experience.

Short branches curving down from the Heart Line suggest short-term relationships.

Chains on the Heart Line represent traumatic relationships. Breaks indicate sudden dramatic endings of relationships. Double

Heart Lines are indicative of a person who is a loyal and devoted partner. See the table opposite for the meaning of other important marks that may occur on the Heart Line.

The Fate Line

The Fate Line (see illustration on page 129) begins its journey at the wrist and travels up the palm toward the Saturn (second) finger. It reflects a person's sense of responsibility. A substantial gap between the Fate Line and the Life Line signifies independence at an early age and indicates a person's desire to leave the nest early.

However, if there are faint lines connecting the Fate Line to the Life Line, this indicates that the person will retain a good relationship with her parents, albeit from a distance.

If the Fate Line begins its journey as part of the Life Line, the person will likely be strongly influenced by her parents' guidance and support early in her career, sometimes becoming part of a family business venture.

If the Fate Line begins inside the Life Line, it indicates that the person could allow her family to influence her choice of career or relationships.

Particular notice should be paid to lines running into and joining the Fate Line. These are called Attachment Lines, because they indicate marriage relationships. When such a line joins the Fate Line low on the palm, it indicates that the person is willing and able to take responsibility for such a commitment early in life.

If the Attachment Line is long before joining the Fate Line, it means there will be a long union before the marriage. The absence of these Attachment Lines does not mean that there is absence of committed relationships, but it does suggest that the person may not be ready for marriage at the time of commitment.

Career changes are indicated by a forked or Y-shaped split in the Fate Line. Crosses, stars, breaks, or islands on the Fate Line are indicative of setbacks to the subject's goals and ambitions (see also the table opposite).

IMPORTANT MARKINGS

Certain important markings, such as crosses, stars, and chains, will appear and disappear on the palms of the hands. They serve as temporary warning signs or herald periods of good fortune.

As a general rule, crosses represent some minor setback. For example, if a cross were to appear on the Life Line, it could be signaling a period of loss of physical energy, because the Life Line represents the life force. If a cross appears on the Head Line, a period of mental fatigue should be expected.

Tiny red dots may appear on one of the Main Lines, but you might need a good magnifying glass to detect them. They are cause for temporary concern. They are saying: stop, look, listen, avoid. When the period of danger is over, they disappear.

Crosses	Crosses on parts of the palm will appear Whenever a time of trouble is near
Squares	Boxes or squares are a sign of protection From danger that lurks from unwanted infection
Chains	Chains that have formed upon any line Are indicating a difficult time
Breaks	Breaks in a line of the palm indicate Short setbacks of a temporary state
Dots	Small dots appearing need special attention These are signs of fate's intervention
Triangles	Signs of a triangle signal despair Do not take chances, be wise and beware
Stars	A star on the Mount of Apollo brings money Sometimes on Venus, a good-looking honey
Grilles	Grilles are quite simply lines in excess Excessive behavior leads to distress
Tassels	Lines that are tasseled mean energy drained When you overdo things there's naught to be gained
Branches or Forked Lines	Improvement is noted when branches arise Drooping branches can mean "sad surprise"
Islands	Problems and islands are one and the same Did you create them? Or is fate to blame?

THE MINOR LINES

While the Main Lines are easy to identify, the Minor Lines very often show a slight difference in place and direction from palm to palm.

The Apollo Line

The Apollo Line, when it is present, indicates a fortunate life for its subject. If it is a full line, it travels from within the Mount of the Moon at the wrist to a point beneath the Apollo (third) finger. However, since the journey of life is seldom completely free of difficulties, the Apollo Line is more likely to appear at irregular intervals and then disappear again; in many hands, it is also difficult to distinguish. Whether the subject decides to use fortunate circumstances of birth, their innate creative talents, or the advantages of a union with another person will be demonstrated by the appearance and condition of this line—a well-defined and long Apollo Line, for instance, shows an uninterrupted successful journey.

A line that begins between the Head and Heart Lines with a faint appearance and ends in a fork indicates a career that loses prestige and financial benefit. An Apollo Line that is well defined but starts late suggests good fortune for a late starter, someone who missed the bus early in life but made up ground with determination and effort.

The absence of this line does not indicate bad luck or lack of success. It is more than likely just a sign of lack of interest in achieving success. Frayed lines, islands, and crosses represent setbacks because of illness or temporary failure (see page 133).

The Simian Line

This unusual sign appears as a straight line across the palm of the hand, combining the Head Line and the Heart Line into one entity. (This peculiar formation has traditionally been known as the Simian Line, although modern palmists are hesitant to use this name, which suggests an ape-like hand.)

The personality traits associated with this line are related to difficulties in determining priorities between the heart and emotions and the practical, logical side of the personality. These people seem to have difficulty separating intellect from emotion or concentrating on both at the same time.

People with this line should settle for nothing less in a partner than someone who can offer an equal amount of intellectual and emotional support, because they find it hard to cope with an uneven balance.

The Marriage Lines

Perhaps because palmistry is such an ancient art, some of the traditional lifestyles and values inspired students of the craft to label some of the lines accordingly. The Lines of Marriage are a typical example of this. Modern palmists are more inclined to refer to these lines as Affection Lines.

The Marriage Lines are situated on the outside edge of the palm between the base of the Mercury (little) finger and the Heart Line. Well-defined lines represent relationships that result in long-term commitments, and faint lines represent relationships that are significant but ultimately just passing influences.

For an approximate idea of timing, measure the distance between the base of the Mercury finger and the Heart Line. The halfway mark should represent the age of about twenty-five years.

Straight, well-defined Marriage Lines without markings indicate a lasting commitment. A Marriage Line ending in a "fork" suggests a sudden ending of the marriage. Many forks on the Marriage Line are associated with a person's persistence in trying to make a difficult marriage work. A Marriage Line that curves up toward the Mercury (little) finger suggests the marriage partner's improved success during the relationship. If the line curves downward, touching or passing through the Heart Line, it foretells a dramatic ending to the marriage—the result of the partner's destiny taking a sudden change of direction.

A fork at the beginning of the Marriage Line (the outside edge) indicates that obstacles and difficulties will cause delays and separation before marriage.

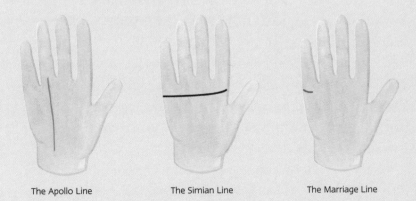

The Apollo Line   The Simian Line   The Marriage Line

The Children Lines

Close scrutiny is necessary in defining the Children Lines, because they can be confused by the lines of stress or worry that sometimes occupy the same space. However, on very close inspection it is possible to identify the number and sex of the children.

The Children Lines are those faint lines that touch or cross the Marriage Line. Child-carers have many faint lines in this area, but they do not touch or cross the Marriage Line.

Straight lines indicate boys; curved lines indicate girls.

If the Children Lines appear to "wander" away from the Marriage Line it suggests a behavioral problem in the child that causes them to want independence too early in life.

The Health Line

Should you experience confusion identifying this line, do not be alarmed, for it does indeed seem to serve a dual purpose: the Health Line appears on the palm during times of sickness, but it also appears on the palms of those who are physical, mental, or spiritual healers. This seems to indicate that its absence on the palm means either freedom from sickness or that the person is not involved with the healing of others.

When it is present, the Health Line generally begins near the Life Line and travels upward, across the palm, to a point on or beneath the Mount of Mercury.

A Health Line that appears broken or frayed denotes periods of ill health for the subject, or periods of responsibility for the health of others, such as aged parents, which in turn takes a toll on the health of the care giver.

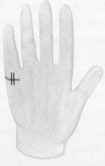

The Children Lines

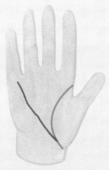

The Health Line

The Girdle of Venus

The Girdle of Venus

There is much debate among palmists about the function of the
Girdle of Venus, a line that extends from between the Jupiter
(index) and Saturn (second) fingers to between the Apollo (third)
and Mercury (little) fingers. Although there is some question as to
the precise meaning of this line, it is safe to say that an unbroken
Girdle of Venus indicates a healthy, sensitive, sensuous nature, while
a broken Girdle of Venus may suggest an overly sensitive and
hysterical disposition.

The Line of Intuition

The Line of Intuition begins low down on the Mount of the Moon
and curves upward into the Mount of Mercury. A long, well-defined
Line of Intuition signifies a person who is very sensitive and gifted
with psychic ability. When the line is faint it has the same meaning,
but to a lesser degree.

The Medical and Teaching Lines

The Medical Lines are above the Heart Line and below the space
between the Apollo (third) and Mercury (little) fingers. They
indicate a vocational inclination toward caring for other people,
especially in the medical field.

These lines should not be confused with the line or lines
beneath the Mercury finger itself, which represent teaching skills.

If the Teaching Lines connect with the Medical Lines, it indicates
that the subject has abilities in the area of spiritual healing and the
teaching of spiritual matters.

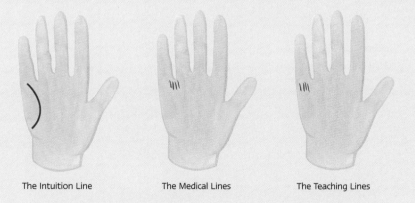

The Intuition Line   The Medical Lines   The Teaching Lines

THE MOUNTS

The mounts—known as the Mounts of Jupiter, Saturn, Apollo, Mercury, Venus, and Moon, and the Upper and Lower Mounts of Mars—are situated in various parts of the palm. They are the over- or underdeveloped sections of the palm, and each is governed by the influence of a particular planet.

These planetary influences are enhanced when the relevant mounts are well developed. Underdeveloped mounts simply suggest that the person does not have the need or desire to use the benefits of those planetary influences at this point in their journey. The person may develop the use of one or more of these influences if and when it becomes advantageous to do so: for instance, a person traveling a creative path in life will not need the aggressive influence of the planet Mars in order to achieve success, whereas a person with a military or political career would benefit from its forceful influence.

Similarly, a person pursuing a career that requires the skills of imagination, writing, teaching, and communication would benefit from the influences of the moon and Mercury. People who change career paths fairly often show evidence of this through well-developed mounts of several planetary influences.

Mount of Jupiter

The Mount of Jupiter represents power, ambition, logic, and ego, and when this mount is well developed, it suggests a personality who is using these qualities to his best advantage. It shows potential for leadership and organizational ability, strong political and religious beliefs, and an authoritarian nature. When the Mount of Jupiter is flat, the subject is unlikely to pursue these ambitions, and if this mount has an overly developed appearance there is possibly an inclination toward bigotry, arrogance, selfishness, and bullying.

Mount of Saturn

The Mount of Saturn represents the serious attitude toward the achievement of material gain and recognition. People with scientific, investigative minds have well-developed Mounts of Saturn. They don't care for trivial pursuits and they don't easily tolerate people governed by their emotions. An overly developed Mount of Saturn indicates a person who will become pessimistic, solitary, and too cautious in their attitude to the journey of life. This is one case,

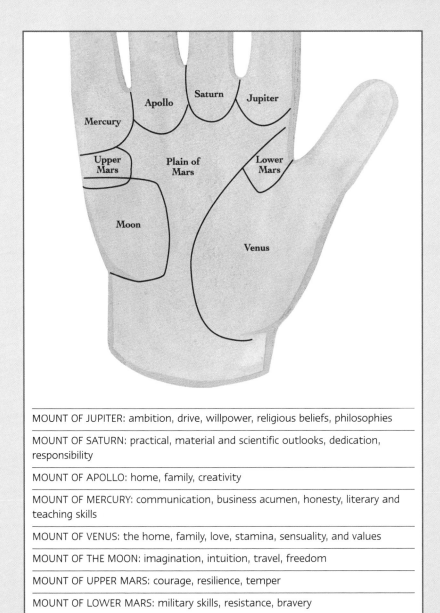

MOUNT OF JUPITER: ambition, drive, willpower, religious beliefs, philosophies

MOUNT OF SATURN: practical, material and scientific outlooks, dedication, responsibility

MOUNT OF APOLLO: home, family, creativity

MOUNT OF MERCURY: communication, business acumen, honesty, literary and teaching skills

MOUNT OF VENUS: the home, family, love, stamina, sensuality, and values

MOUNT OF THE MOON: imagination, intuition, travel, freedom

MOUNT OF UPPER MARS: courage, resilience, temper

MOUNT OF LOWER MARS: military skills, resistance, bravery

therefore, where an underdeveloped mount is a plus: a flat Mount of Saturn represents a person who, although governed by logic and strong ideas, nevertheless has an approachable personality. Careers that are attractive to these people include medicine, science, and economics.

Mount of Apollo

The Mount of Apollo, governed by the sun, represents creativity, family, growth, expansion, and good fortune. A well-developed Mount of Apollo indicates a person who appreciates beauty, nature, creativity, the arts, children, family, and animals. Special attention is given to the markings on this mount because it can herald good luck, success, and financial gains.

A Mount of Apollo that is excessively developed suggests hedonistic behavior, the result of too much good fortune. An underdeveloped Mount of Apollo indicates that, for the time being, the subject's interests and expectations in these areas are not active. Famous successful people have well-developed Mounts of Apollo with distinctive markings.

Mount of Mercury

The Mount of Mercury is associated with communication, self-expression, literary skills, and personal relationships. A well-developed Mount of Mercury suggests an approachable, confident personality who is a good mediator, teacher, or journalist. A flat or underdeveloped mount indicates a shy personality, someone who has poor business skills and difficulty expressing themselves.

Mount of Venus

The Mount of Venus represents emotional and physical energy—love, creativity, and drive. A well-developed Mount of Venus suggests a personality who knows how to appreciate and enjoy life to the fullest. These people are sensual and sociable beings with a taste for good food, wine, good music, and good humor. However, if this mount is too soft in appearance, it may indicate a personality prone to overindulgence. A flat, tight Mount of Venus suggests a personality who lacks stamina and seems uninterested in pursuing life's pleasures.

Mount of the Moon

The Mount of the Moon represents imagination, creativity, and travel. People with a well-developed Mount of the Moon have good creative and imaginative skills, and are attracted to and skilled at water sports. A flat or underdeveloped Mount of the Moon indicates a person who dislikes to travel and does not possess a vivid imagination.

Upper Mount of Mars

The Upper Mount of Mars represents courage and aggression. When this mount is well developed it indicates a confrontational personality who can deal with a crisis in a practical manner. Those with an underdeveloped Upper Mount of Mars tend to dislike confrontation.

Lower Mount of Mars

A well-developed Lower Mount of Mars is a sign of an aggressive nature. These people seem to enjoy making a battle out of life's journey, attacking life rather than submitting to it. The apparent absence of a Lower Mount of Mars suggests that the person will do her best to avoid volatile conditions.

SAMPLE DESTINY—MADELINE

At a glance you can see that Madeline has a "full hand" (many fine lines); the hand is conic-shaped with a long thumb, a long Mercury finger, and finger phalanges that are well proportioned. All of this tells us at once that here we have an idealistic, sensitive person with creative instincts (the conic shape). The fullness of her palm (many lines) suggests that she is emotional and suffers from a nervous disposition, her highly developed imagination often causing her to expect disappointments before they arrive.

The many lines also suggest that she has faced a lot of emotional

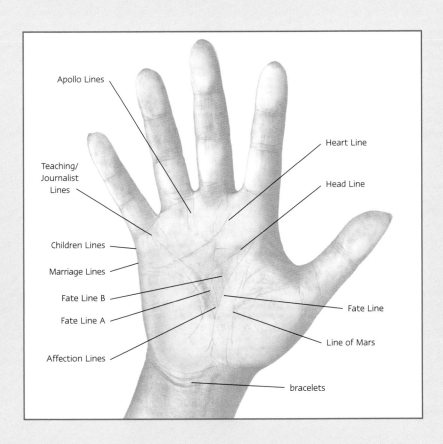

challenges in personal relationships, and that these have caused her to become suspicious of people's intentions and expectations. But the positive influences of a full hand will encourage her to develop her creative and artistic talents, supported by the strong lines under her Apollo finger, which will eventually give her the confidence to achieve her goals, especially those she hopes to achieve through her literary skills—these are shown by the "writer's fork" on the end of her Head Line and the long Mercury (little) finger, which guarantees her the gift of self-expression and the acquisition of journalistic skills.

This long Mercury finger with its long first and second phalanges further ensures that Madeline is destined to fulfill her artistic and literary ambitions. The fact that this finger also has a tendency to lean toward the Apollo finger suggests that she has the ability and tenacity to pursue her dreams. The flexible, long thumb reinforces this idea, indicating an innate staying power, enthusiasm, and a logical, rational attitude.

Madeline's Life Line begins its journey high up on the palm near the Mount of Jupiter (representing ambition), and travels in a well-defined condition around a developed Mount of Venus to a point around the age of about seventy years, where it divides into a fork (showing a desire to gather experience from home and far away).

During her formative years (birth to fifteen years) the Life Line and Head Line cross paths, forming an island; this indicates that some trauma was experienced during this period. A succession of crosses and squares sitting between the Life and Head Lines are indicative of difficult times during her twenties and thirties, which have caused her both mental and physical exhaustion. But the squares (protection from danger), plus the well-defined Line of Mars, indicate that she will overcome these challenges.

The Head Line on Madeline's hand is well developed and long, without the disruption of breaks or islands, and curves gently down into the Mount of the Moon. This signifies a well-adjusted, level-headed personality who is also blessed with imagination, idealism, romance, and creativity, proving that even at this stage every line, mount, shape, and marking arise confirming her talent.

Madeline has a curved Heart Line, which shows that she is an emotional person with a lot of love to give. Her Heart Line begins near the Mount of Jupiter, indicating that she will not settle for less than what she needs in a relationship. The combination of a curved Head Line and a curved Heart Line means that Madeline will not easily forget the details of her relationships—the good and the bad will both be remembered. People who have curved Main Lines can be vulnerable to partners with jealous or dominating natures.

The Heart Line should now be divided into the three sections of "A," affection; "B," emotion; and "C," health. The "A" section of Madeline's Heart Line is forked at the beginning, implying that she will have a practical but caring attitude toward her partner. The "B" section shows a branch sloping downward from the line, indicating a disappointing result of a relationship beginning in her early thirties. She obviously tried to maintain this relationship, despite all its faults, since no break appears until much later along the Heart Line, when a dot followed by a succession of chained islands indicate that the relationship ended in unhappiness due to cruelty by Madeline's partner. The "C" section is entirely made up of a feathered jagged look, indicating health problems connected with the lungs.

Madeline appears to have a double Fate Line. The position and appearance of these lines—one starting on the Mount of the Moon, crossing the Head Line and joining a downward-sloping branch from the Heart Line (indicating a self-motivated attitude up to that point) and the other starting from a point on the Life Line, crossing the Head Line and ending on a point parallel to the other Fate Line—strongly suggest that because of the interference caused by an unfortunate choice of partner, the growth and expansion of an otherwise successful career are thwarted. However, these two Fate Lines are also made up of square formations, which will give Madeline protection from unscrupulous business partners. Another short line shooting upward from the Fate Line to the Heart Line indicates that Madeline will create her own business, working mainly from home.

Madeline has one only strong Marriage Line—it occurs after age forty and produces or "inherits" two children (a girl and a boy).

Summary

This gifted, creative, intelligent person will eventually gain reward and recognition for her effort and talent, and even though the first half of her life is plagued by emotional trauma from family and personal relationships, she has the courage and determination to confront her problems, eventually turning the lessons learned from these experiences into advantages, therefore making the second half of her life fulfilling and rewarding.

PLAYING CARDS

Using an ordinary deck of playing cards to predict the past, present, and future events of your destiny is an age-old custom that has proved to be both a popular and accurate method of fortune-telling.

Using cards for fortune-telling purposes is often referred to as cartomancy. Students of this craft are immediately impressed by the easy technique of this type of divination, and professional readers continue to experiment and improve on a variety of creative ways of transforming the pictures and patterns of a layout into an accurate account of a person's destiny.

Each of the four suits (diamonds, clubs, hearts, spades) represents an aspect of life, and each individual card has a specific meaning. Groups and pairs of cards with the same numerical value are taken into account for their potential impact.

Cartomancy should be awarded the same respect as any other means of serious psychic divination. It is best practiced during the most potent period of the day: the early evening or twilight. This is generally regarded as the "bewitching hour"—the mysterious occult vibration is thought to peak at this time.

All that remains is that you commit to memory the following interpretations. Begin your exploration of this kind of fortune-telling with the "7 Up" method, which means you use only those cards with a numerical value of seven or more plus the "court" cards (Kings, Queens, Jacks) and the Ace. This is an easy and accurate method that can be mastered in a reasonably short time.

An ordinary deck of playing cards can also be put to good use in developing your psychic ability because you can use your intuitive skills to interpret the various combinations and layouts. You can be as creative as you wish in finding new ways to interpret time and events. See also "Tarot," pages 166–177.

HOW TO START

Pick up a clean pack of cards and hold them in your hands for several minutes while you think of a question you would like to have answered. Next, shuffle the cards and keep asking your question. The harder you focus, the more accurate your reading will be. When you feel ready, deal six cards off the top onto a clean cloth or table. Place them in six different positions, well apart from each other, and face up. Each position represents one of the following:

- Yourself
- Your family
- Your friends

- What you expect
- What you don't expect
- The outcome

Shuffle the cards again and deal another six cards off the top, placing each to one side of one of the six cards already on the cloth or table. Repeat this one more time so that you have three cards for each position.

Sample interpretation

YOURSELF: There is a change ahead, which has legal connotations, but it's a good outcome because both the Tens are red.

YOUR FAMILY: Three Sevens. Three Sevens mean news of a birth, but the Seven of Spades suggests that there will be a slight delay.

YOUR FRIENDS: Two Eights and a Seven. Two Eights suggest some mild gossip about a financial issue. This position belongs to your friends—the problem is theirs, not yours.

WHAT YOU EXPECT: The Nine of Hearts is an emotional wish fulfilled, the Eight of Hearts is a celebration about that wish, and the Ace of Diamonds represents either a letter or a ring. Given the other two cards, it would be safe to interpret this card as representing a ring.

WHAT YOU DON'T EXPECT: The three Queens show that there is gossip bordering on scandal. But since this position belongs to what you are not expecting to happen, this drama may not be about you, though you will be drawn into it.

THE OUTCOME: Two Nines are always auspicious. The outcome over the next three months is very favorable for friends, finances, and emotions, but the Ten of Spades signifies a delay.

THE MEANING OF THE SUITS

The suit of Hearts represents emotional issues: love and romance and family ties. The positive and negative influences that affect these aspects of life are examined by this suit. Hearts also represent the water signs: Cancer, Scorpio, and Pisces.

The suit of Clubs represents communication, energy, the environment, and the positive and negative influences affecting these aspects of life. Clubs also represent the fire signs: Aries, Leo, and Sagittarius.

The suit of Diamonds represents the material world—money, business, and the positive and negative influences affecting these aspects of life. Diamonds also represent the earth signs: Taurus, Virgo, and Capricorn.

The suit of Spades represents health, both mental and physical, and the difficulties we must learn to deal with in life. Spades also represent the air signs: Aquarius, Gemini, and Libra.

GROUPS OF SAME VALUE IN A LAYOUT	
Aces:	4 total success—3 business negotiations—2 marriage
Kings:	4 reward for effort—3 promotion—2 minor reward
Queens:	4 gossip, slander—3 idle gossip—2 nosy neighbors
Jacks:	4 volatile arguments—3 friction—2 slight altercation
Tens:	4 good prospects—3 serious money problems—2 small financial gain
Nines:	4 great good fortune—3 wish fulfilled—2 pleasant surprise
Eights:	4 anxiety, confusion—3 worry, stress—2 love affair
Sevens:	4 public confrontation—3 unexpected pregnancy—2 lies, deceit

INDIVIDUAL CARDS

A	Hearts	Mutual love and happiness
K	Hearts	A fair-complexioned, fair-minded adult male
Q	Hearts	A fair-complexioned, affectionate female
J	Hearts	An honest, dependable young man
10	Hearts	Success and good fortune
9	Hearts	A wish fulfilled
8	Hearts	An unexpected visit or present
7	Hearts	A fickle admirer
A	Clubs	Some large investments you will wish to make
K	Clubs	A kind-hearted man—dark-haired
Q	Clubs	A friendly dark-haired woman who is inclined to gossip though not maliciously
J	Clubs	A friendly young man with dark hair. Everyone's favorite, but can be a rogue
10	Clubs	Success in business
9	Clubs	A large amount of money—sometimes a wealthy marriage
8	Clubs	A small monetary gain
7	Clubs	A dark-haired young girl who is friendly
A	Diamonds	A new message indicating change
K	Diamonds	A man in a position of authority and power—fair or gray-haired
Q	Diamonds	A frivolous female who takes what she wants—blond
J	Diamonds	An official young man—someone in uniform
10	Diamonds	Change for the better connected with financial gain
9	Diamonds	New business deal
8	Diamonds	Work-related card—could mean a new job
7	Diamonds	An argument over money matters
A	Spades	Great misfortune or even death
K	Spades	A legal representative
Q	Spades	Widowed or divorced woman
J	Spades	An enemy—jealous and volatile
10	Spades	Worry—vexation—sometimes illness
9	Spades	Near-fatal illness or accident
8	Spades	Misfortune—danger—temptations
7	Spades	Bad advice

RUNES

Runes are sacred symbols that were used for magical practices, including fortune-telling, by such ancient civilizations as the Celtic and Germanic peoples. Various runic systems evolved and three codifications emerged: the Elder Futhark or Fupark (twenty-four runes), the Younger Futhark or Norse system (sixteen runes), and the Anglo-Saxon Futhork (thirty-three runes). We will focus on the twenty-four-rune system to illustrate how to use runes as a divinatory tool.

There are a number of rune sets available in New Age shops. However, you may wish to make your own set and develop your own understanding of how to interpret the runes by using the interpretation table on pages 150–151.

Runes were traditionally carved in stone, bone, or wood. To make wooden runes, cut out and sand twenty-four pieces of wood, each approximately an inch square. Smooth out the edges so that they are well rounded.

Consider using a timber that resonates with prophecy and magical purposes, such as balsa wood, cedar, or pine. These woods are rather soft, so you will be able to impress the runic images on the wood before carefully painting over the indentation with acrylic or enamel paint. Enamel paint is much more hardwearing than acrylic, and is available in a range of colors from any good craft store. Use two or three coats of silver, black, red, or gold enamel for the runic symbol itself.

If you would like to make clay runes, either out of terra-cotta clay or special clay that can be fired in an ordinary oven, consider using a reddish-colored clay. Use a blunt knife to impress the straight lines of the runes into the clay.

Stone runes are among the simplest to make. First you need to acquire or find twenty-four smooth pebbles or stones of roughly the same size. Then just paint the runes onto the stones. It is best to use enamel paints on stone so that the symbols don't wear off.

Once you have finished making your runes, you might want to make or purchase a drawstring bag made from soft, natural fabric to keep your runes in.

USING RUNES TO INTERPRET YOUR ANSWERS

After you have acquired or made your set of runes, take some time to become acquainted with each rune. You may wish to do a meditation on each rune at the same time each day for twenty-four days. Get yourself a journal to be used only for your rune work and write in it the various interpretations that you can find about each rune. Then add your own insights after each meditation session.

Traditionally, after holding the bag of runes in your hands and thinking of a question to which you want an answer, the runes are thrown directly out of a bag onto a white cloth. Depending on how they are grouped and whether the runic symbols are upright or reversed, a reading can commence.

A simpler way of using the runes is just to take one rune out of the bag to answer your question. Use the table on pages 150–151 to see if you can interpret the rune to apply to your particular situation and question.

Another way of using the runes is to do a three-rune spread, which simply requires you to take three runes out of the bag. The first rune indicates the issue that you are dealing with. The second rune signifies what is blocking you from achieving a solution to your issue; it could also give you some indication of what you need to do to resolve your current issue. The third rune represents the outcome of this action.

A SIMPLE INVOCATION

The great Norse god Odin was believed to have derived knowledge of the magic of the runes while he was in a trance, hanging from Yggdrasil (the Nordic tree of knowledge). If you wish to add further power to your runic divination, say the following invocation before you cast or choose your runes:

Odin, great God of knowledge,

I ask for your insight and help.

Share your wisdom of the runes with me.

RUNE INTERPRETATION

The table below lists the twenty-four commonly used runes of the Elder Futhark. Each rune is accompanied by its corresponding number, name, image, and interpretation.

NUMBER	NAME	RUNE	INTERPRETATION
1	Fehu	ᚠ	This refers to new beginnings in terms of a family, or embarkation upon a new project or different career path.
2	Uruz	ᚢ	This refers to the power and courage needed to bring a new project or venture to completion.
3	Thurisaz	ᚦ	This refers to unexpected but minor problems and delays in your projects or ventures, such as the emergence of a new competitor or petty jealousies.
4	Ansuz	ᚨ	This refers to a project or venture being protected by an older mentor or friend who is able to give you inspiration and guidance.
5	Raidho	ᚱ	This refers to changes, such as finding a new home or workplace, or unexpected travel that proves to be very rewarding.
6	Kaunaz	ᚲ	This refers to your ability to transform the situation in a creative way or suggests the transformation of a friendship into a passionate relationship.
7	Gebo	ᚷ	This is an indication of entry into a favorable marriage or business partnership, and can refer to being rewarded for your past endeavors.
8	Wunjo	ᚹ	This is a symbol of happiness and joy, indicating a prosperous and harmonious period of your life.
9	Hagalaz	ᚺ	This indicates that you require protection against unexpected delays and problems and that you may need to reevaluate your goals in life.
10	Naudhiz	ᚾ	This refers to taking action only after considering the full ramifications; you must look beyond the surface of a person's actions.
11	Isa	ᛁ	This is symbolic of isolation. You may be in a transitory phase of your life, so you must be patient before your goal is reached.

NUMBER	NAME	RUNE	INTERPRETATION
12	Jera		This represents the completion of a project or the finalization of an important contract that will lead to a comfortable lifestyle.
13	Eihwaz		This is an indication that you are undergoing a trying time at present and that you will need to make new long-term plans.
14	Perdhro		This means that you will be doing a lot more socializing and entertaining in this period, which also signals unexpected financial gains.
15	Elhaz		This refers to a situation where you will feel undermined; you will need to stick to what you believe in to get through the situation.
16	Sowilo		This refers to the culmination of all the goods things of life—romance, health, finances, and success in studies.
17	Tiwaz		This means that you will have success in implementing your ambitious plans or consummating a new passionate relationship.
18	Berkano		This refers to new growth in terms of your creativity or fertility, leading to a long-term commitment to a relationship or a business venture.
19	Ehwaz		This represents changes in your work life or where you are living, possibly leading you to travel.
20	Mannaz		This refers to an initiation into a new way of life—into feeling confident enough to stand on your own two feet.
21	Laguz		This refers to opportunities arising for travel—either for work or pleasure. This travel may lead you to feel temporarily disoriented, but the journey will end successfully.
22	Ingwaz		This represents a period of gestation and consolidation that means you have succeeded in finishing a particular cycle in your life, and should take a well-earned break.
23	Dagaz		This refers to a sudden change of attitude that leads you into a new lifestyle or career path.
24	Othalaz		This represents the gaining of material possessions through inheritance or a close bonding of family members.

S

SCRIVENING

Scrivening or scrying is a method of fortune-telling by which a
fortune-teller is able to see shapes and images that foretell the future
in a variety of surfaces such as water, ice, smoke, or the reflective
surfaces of a mirror, crystal, or crystal ball (see pages 80–81).

As a variation, certain substances like ink, food, or wax
(see pages 182–183) are dropped into a bowl of water and an
interpretation of the future is intuited from the shapes formed by
those substances in the water.

An advanced method of fortune-telling that requires strong
meditation and clairvoyant skills is the ability to see images and
symbols while meditating over a bowl (preferably a crystal bowl) of
water. To do this, scriveners set up a psychic ambience by burning
two white candles and essential oils such as frankincense and
myrrh to heighten their fortune-telling abilities. Then, in quiet
meditation, they concentrate on the crystal bowl of water.

Images, sometimes of a smoky nature, will slowly emerge,
becoming clearer as the time of meditation increases. Faces,
symbols, scenery—one or all of these images will take shape. Then
scriveners listen intently to their intuition, feeling their way around
the imagery to form a story.

The water may also create a warm or cold sensation, or a calm
or turbulent impression may be felt. The water will be clear, but
may give the impression of murkiness. An example of this might be:

*I see an old man (a face) causing you problems (turbulent waters).
He is being dishonest about something (murky water), but things will
be sorted out satisfactorily and peace will be restored (calm water).*

A scrivener is able to interpret the signals so well because he or she
has an unrestrained or uncluttered mind. While psychics of all kinds
are born with a particular sensitivity, they all still need to undergo
rigorous training and practice in order to achieve real results.

SCRIVENING USING WATER

All scrivening must be performed in a darkened room, preferably at night. If possible, always cast a psychic circle before doing any scrivening (see pages 56–59). If you have a special psychic space set up (see pages 52–55), consider hanging dark curtains on the windows and dark fabrics on the walls. The darker your space is, the easier it will be to see the images in the water.

Fill a crystal bowl with fresh water and set it in the darkest spot of your psychic space, away from any window or doorway. When you have set up your space and are sitting comfortably, focus on your breathing or simply gaze at the water's surface, resting your mind and letting the thoughts of the day float by. Feel your mind become still. Ask your question about the future and continue to gaze at the water. You may at the same time observe your breath quietly moving in and out of your nostrils.

Some water scriveners like to move a hand over the water as a way of helping break the eyes' gaze, triggering the mind to see beyond the actual surface of the water and into a psychic dimension. If you are having particular difficulty, you may wish to try covering your head and the bowl with a sheer black cloth.

You may start to see clouds forming over the water as you continue to meditate on the water's surface. As shapes or pictures form in the clouds above the water, try not to focus on these images too hard—if you do, they will tend to slip away. As the images begin to emerge, try to focus your eyes on a point midway between you and the bowl. This should help you maintain your connection with the images.

SCRIVENING USING A MIRROR

All you need for this fortune-telling technique is a mirror. It can be any kind of mirror, from a new one purchased especially for this purpose to one that you have had in the family for so many years that the backing has started to craze and distort. Use your intuition as to what kind of mirror you would like to use. An old mirror may make you feel that since it has reflected many years of life, it has some innate quality of wisdom.

You may wish to have the mirror framed. Align the frame of your scrying mirror with the element that resonates with your date of birth (see pages 44–45 and 62–63). If you have a choice, you may choose to frame the mirror with wood (if you are an earth element) or metal (if you are an air element), or choose a frame that is colored red (if you are a fire element) or blue (if you are a water element).

In a darkened room, position the mirror so that it is reflecting a blank surface, preferably a dark-colored wall or wall-hanging. Follow the same techniques as for water scrivening to set up your scrivening session.

When your mirror is not in use, always store it covered with a dark cloth. Try not to expose the mirror to sunlight— it is believed that this will undermine the ability of the mirror to help you see beyond the physical world.

SCRIVENING TIP

Try this ancient form of scrivening. All you need is a fresh, running stream and a mirror, preferably one that has not been cleaned for a while. Ask a question, particularly about a person or about someone you would like to find, such as: "Who will I marry?" or "Who stole all my CDs?" With this question in mind, dip the mirror into the water and pull it out. While standing in the shade, see if you can distinguish the face of a person on the surface of the mirror.

SCRIVENING USING SMOKE

There are many ways to create the smoke you need to answer a question about the future or to have a prophetic vision. Traditionally, many gruesome rituals were performed so that the smoke emanating from carcasses or skulls could be read to foretell the future.

There are now other methods, methods that don't require the death of an animal, of creating the right atmosphere for smoke or air scrivening. For instance, you may burn a certain incense stick, cone, or charcoal block and, in a meditative state, observe the images and shapes that form as the incense burns.

Choose incense that complements the question you seek to have answered. If you wish to see visions of the future, try frankincense or myrrh incense. If you wish to see an image of your future love, try rose geranium, jasmine, musk, or patchouli incense.

If you want an indication of your future financial standing, burn incense sticks containing cedar or lavender. If you wish to find out who are your enemies, consider burning rosemary incense. If this fortune-telling technique appeals to you, experiment with different scents and brands of incense to find the right blend for the right occasion.

Another way of creating the right type of smoke for your scrivening is to burn crumpled plain paper in a pot half filled with sand. (Never use newspaper—the smell is quite acrid.) Include a piece of paper on which you have written the question you wish the visions in the smoke to answer. You may also include a scattering of a visionary herb, such as mugwort, to help you see your answer.

SCRIVENING TIP

Make sure that the space you use for smoke or air scrivening is well ventilated and that you are protected from any drafts. Also make sure that the doors and window sills do not rattle.

SPELLS

A spell is essentially a ritualized method of focusing the mind to help achieve a particular purpose or to find out the answer to a particular question.

The key to spell craft is to decide what you want to achieve by concentrating on the appropriate image or words. It is said that by the sheer act of concentration on what you wish to have or to know you are opening an "astral doorway" to a new reality where what you want to bring into being or what you want to know will actually manifest. But your intention must be strong and clear.

When you are using spell craft as a fortune-telling technique it is important to only ask one question at a time. Work out precisely what you want to know. The sample spells on the following pages will show you how spells can be used to find out all kinds of things in a number of different areas.

Once you get the idea, you will be able to devise your own spells for getting a precise answer to your question. If you simply want a "yes" or "no" answer to a question, try the fortune-telling spell on the opposite page.

One of the major challenges of spell craft is to prophesize the future. The spell on page 158 will give you a simple and safe way of tapping into the "universal subconscious" for the purpose of divining the future. This will take some practice; keep in mind that the more developed your psychic ability, the easier it will be for you to see visions about the future and, most important, to accurately interpret what they mean.

For answers concerning the success of a business venture, try the spell on page 159; for questions about your love life, try the spells on pages 160–161.

FORTUNE-TELLING SPELL

This is an excellent spell to give you a simple yes or no answer to a straightforward question about your future. Will I get that promotion? Will I become a success? This spell will get you in the right frame of mind to get an accurate response to your question regardless of what you hope the answer will be. If you are new to fortune-telling, you may wish to do this spell with a friend, so that you answer each other's question, without prejudice.

What do I need?

• A sheet of paper
• A pen
• A piece of jasper (preferably brown)
• A pendulum

When should I do this spell?

On a Monday

What should I do?

Write down on the sheet of paper the question that you would like to have answered. Go outside with your stone and find a patch of ground to stand on, preferably barefoot. Feel the energy of the earth under your feet, then bend down and push the jasper into the earth. Imagine the energy coming up through your feet spiraling down through your arms and the stone into the ground. This is an important grounding exercise. Concentrate on the flow of energy through you. Do not think of your question.

When you feel grounded, place the jasper in a left pocket and come inside to do the rest of the spell. Sit at a table that will allow you to comfortably rest your elbow while holding the pendulum between your thumb and forefinger. The pendulum should swing freely near the surface of the table.

First ask the pendulum which way is "yes." This will differ for each pendulum and each person using it. Then ask it which way is "no." Place the piece of paper under the pendulum and ask your question, concentrating on the flow of energy within you. This will ensure that the pendulum gives the right answer without being influenced by your fears or desires concerning the outcome.

A SIMPLE, SAFE PROPHESY SPELL

There are many traditional ways for preparing yourself to see
prophetic visions; some include consuming hallucinogenic
substances and sniffing foul-smelling herbs. We will instead use
dream visions to help us see into the state of the future.

What do I need?

- A cloth pouch filled with dried mugwort
- A dream journal and a black pen placed on a bedside table
- A precious stone, such as a small sapphire; if you have no access
  to such a stone use a semiprecious azurite

When should I do this spell?

During a full moon

What should I do?

Place the cloth pouch under the pillow and, in your dream journal,
write that you wish to see in the future. Because the future that our
mind presents to us is sometimes simply a reflection of our fears
and desires, we need to tap into a form of energy higher than
ourselves before we do this writing.

For this spell, we will connect with the "universal
subconscious"—a powerful form of energy that surrounds us,
knows all, and sees all.

To help you connect with this higher form of energy, hold the
stone in your left hand as you lie in bed and visualize the energy of
the stone—a deep blue stream of energy—leading both down into
the earth from which it came and up into the heavens, and there
connecting with a white layer of psychic energy surrounding the
earth (representing the "universal subconscious").

Keep this visualization in your mind and chant the following
words until you fall asleep:

If it is in my highest good to know,
Help me see into the future purely
Free from my fears and desires

Upon waking, immediately write
down the visions that you had
during your dream state. To
strengthen the visions, practice
this spell on the next three
full moons.

A SPELL TO FIND OUT IF I WILL BE SUCCESSFUL IN MY BUSINESS VENTURE

You can get an early indication if your business venture is a success or not using a coin. Use an ordinary coin that you have earned through your own skill. As soon as your paycheck has cleared, go to the bank and withdraw some money that includes the highest denomination coin that you can get. Use one of these coins for this spell and any other money spells you cast to attract money to you (keep this coin wrapped in green cloth).

What do I need?

- The World card from your
  favorite tarot deck (XXI of the
  Major Arcana)
- A coin
- A document or item that represents your
  business venture, such as a contract,
  business plan, or picture
- A piece of green cloth, big enough to
  wrap the three items above in

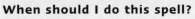

When should I do this spell?

On a Saturday

What should I do?

At dawn, take the World card (which will represent success and completion of a financial venture in this spell), the coin, and your contract, business plan, picture or some symbol of the object of your business venture, and wrap all three in the green cloth, which psychically represents monetary issues and growth. Place this package in a safe place—somewhere elevated, such as the mantelpiece or a high shelf.

Do not touch this package during the day. At twilight of the same day, take the package from its resting place and carry it to a spot where you won't be disturbed. Unwrap the package and think that you would like to know whether the business venture will be successful.

Toss the coin. If it lands heads, the answer is yes. If the coin lands tails, the answer is no.

Don't forget to return the tarot card to its deck as soon as possible after doing this spell.

A SPELL TO FIND OUT THE NAME OF
MY OWN TRUE LOVE

There are a great many traditional spells for finding out the name of your true love. After casting this spell, you may be surprised by the name that comes through. Maybe it is someone you know already but have absolutely no interest in.

Once you have worked out the name of your true love, you can flip a coin to ask whether you already have met your true love—heads is yes and tails is no.

What do I need?

- Four drops of rose geranium essential oil
- A tea light
- An oil burner
- A box of matches
- A sharp paring knife
- One apple
- A metal bowl to catch the peelings

When should I do this spell?

On a Friday

What should I do?

Measure out the essential oil, light the oil burner, and sit in a comfortable chair with the bowl at your feet and the knife and the apple beside you. Place the oil burner near you so that you can smell the scent and see the tea light burning.

Concentrate on the smell of rose geranium and start consciously breathing in for a count of four and out for a count of four. Feel that you are letting go of all your everyday concerns and focus your mind on finding out the name of your true love.

When you feel focused and calm, pick up the apple and the paring knife and say:

With this knife I shall carve out the first letter of my true love's name.

Peel the apple with your right hand if you are right-handed, your left hand if you are left-handed. Keep the line of peel unbroken as long as possible. When the peel breaks, allow it to land in the bowl. See if the shape of the peel forms a letter.

Even if you cannot discern a letter, concentrate on the shape of the peel. The first name that pops into your head will be the name of your true love.

A SPELL TO FIND OUT WHETHER A RELATIONSHIP WILL LAST

The spell below will help you tap into your own instincts about whether or not your relationship has a chance, and will help guide you toward enjoying the relationship you have or finding one that will suit you even better.

What do I need?

- The Lovers card from your favorite tarot deck (VI of the Major Arcana)
- Your journal
- Four drops of cinnamon essential oil
- An oil burner
- A tea light
- A box of matches

When should I do this spell?

On a Friday evening

What should I do?

Gather your tools and ingredients and find a safe and comfortable place where you will not be disturbed. Set up the oil burner, tea light, and the essential oil. Light the candle and breathe in the scent of cinnamon.

Focus on your breathing and feel yourself letting go of your daily worries. Focus on the Lovers card. Allow yourself to examine the image on the card in great detail. Feel as if you are falling into the image.

In this relaxed state of mind, ask the following question:

Will this relationship last?

Continue looking at the card and listen to or watch, in a detached manner, any message, advice, or images that come to your mind. Write these down in your journal. Do not analyze them; just keep writing down anything that comes to your mind. Keep going until you feel ready to stop. Now ask:

What do I need to do to make this relationship last for the benefit of both myself and [insert name]?

Again focus on the card and write down any advice that comes to your mind. Take three deep breaths and turn the tarot card face down. Read what you have written in your journal and sift through the information. You may be surprised by the information you have been given. Above all, honor what your intuition has told you.

STONE CASTING

Semiprecious stones can pick up subtle vibrations around you and help answer your questions about your world, your friends, and your relatives. Because they have a crystalline structure, stones are able to collect and emit electromagnetic energy. In ancient times, crystals were considered invaluable for use in healing and prayer, and to increase spiritual connection.

Using stones to tell your future is one of the easiest methods of fortune-telling. This is because you can tailor your fortune-telling system to suit the type of stones you resonate with. Before doing any stone casting you need to become attuned to each stone you wish to use for this fortune-telling technique.

When choosing crystals, use your intuition. Look at all the crystals available and choose the one or ones you feel most drawn to. Keep a list of stones that you collect and their psychic properties (you may have to research some of them). Here are some of the more popular stones:

Agates are members of the chalcedony family of crystals. They are found in various colors and are translucent. They represent stable energy and improved self-awareness.

Amethyst is violet to purple in color and has a calming energy. It increases your powers of intuition and your clarity of mind.

Aquamarine is a blue-green stone; it signifies a reduction in negativity and may indicate that courage is needed to develop your creativity.

Carnelian, like agate, is part of the chalcedony family, and is a type of quartz that is available in abundance. Its colors generally range from red to orange, but it can sometimes exhibit a dark brown hue. It represents positive motivation and the lessening of stress and anxiety.

Emeralds are from the beryl family of stones, and can be found in colors ranging from pale to very deep green. The emerald is believed to be the stone of true love and may resonate with people from the healing professions. This stone also represents good self-esteem and spiritual growth.

Lapis lazuli is a deep blue stone that was used in ancient Egypt for decoration and spiritual rituals. It represents spiritual enlightenment and the understanding of universal truths.

Moonstones are milky, translucent stones with flashes of pale blue or green. Another balancing crystal, the moonstone signifies strong intuition and logic and acts to balance emotions.

Quartz crystals encompass a large group of stones made mostly of silicon dioxide. Clear quartz represents healing. All types of quartz crystals contain a beautiful energy for increasing emotional peace and wisdom, and they signify a positive outcome.

Rose quartz is a crystal infused with a soft pink color. It contains a gentle energy and signifies love and compassion.

Sapphires are mostly deep blue in color but can also be found in gray, black, yellow, or green. This mystical stone represents good fortune, creativity, and a peaceful time ahead.

Smoky quartz, as the name suggests, is a translucent crystal of a smoky brown color. This crystal signifies the emergence of new ideas after a bout of depression.

Tiger's eye is a glossy brown stone with golden stripes. It represents self-confidence, and reminds us that we have inner resources that will help us cope with difficult issues. It also indicates that our ideas will become reality.

Topaz is a golden yellow or brown stone (occasionally green or blue). This stone, like the sun, represents healing and new inspiration in dealing with difficult people.

Tourmaline stones are a large group of stones including black, blue, green, red, opalized, watermelon, and cat's eye tourmaline. These stones indicate that we will gain the insight to dispel the negativity in our lives.

Turquoise is a beautiful stone that ranges from sky blue to bright blue to green-blue. It represents friendship, improved communication, or success in overcoming an illness.

STONE CASTING TO FIND OUT IF SOMEONE LOVES YOU

There are several ways you can use stones to find out if someone loves you. Choose stones that represent the emotions. If you are trying to find out about your love life and friendships, choose stones that resonate with different kinds of relationships. You may wish to choose a deep red tourmaline to resonate with an uninhibited new sexual adventure, or a pale rose quartz to signify loyal friendship.

The color of the stone is usually a good indicator of the type of love that a person may have for you. White usually symbolizes a

platonic friendship, pink a harmonious friendship, and red a strong physical attraction. A clear quartz crystal could signify that a person has no special feelings for you, while a black stone may symbolize that a person does not like you at all.

The surface texture of a stone may also signify a particular emotional state. If the stone is in a raw, unpolished state, for instance, this may mean that someone loves you but doesn't know it yet. A stone polished into a smooth pebble but with some dents still showing may mean that the person loves you but is still getting over an earlier emotional crisis and not ready to express their love. If a stone is heart-shaped, this may be an indication that the person loves you and is ready to connect with you.

You will need to rely on your intuition to discover what each stone means to you.

You can also find a specific stone to represent yourself and other stones to symbolize the people around you, including the people

---

STONE-GATHERING TIP

If you love the look and feel of stones, and wish to further explore this fascinating form of fortune-telling, keep your collection of stones, including any new ones, in a box lined with natural fabric, such as cotton, silk, flax, or hemp. Before storing your new stones, cleanse them with salty or running water to remove any negative vibrations.

you wish to know better. To find these stones, go to your favorite supplier and pick the first stone you touch or see while thinking of a particular person. Do the same for all your favorite people, making a careful note of which stone represents which person.

To do a simple stone casting, gather up the stones representing your favorite people. Include a stone that represents yourself and another stone that represents an unknown person, someone you do not know yet. Mix all these stones in a sturdy cloth bag. Hold the bag closed in your hands, and ask to see the person who will be your next love. Throw the stones out of the bag, and see which stone lands nearest to you. This stone represents your next love.

If it happens to be the stone that represents someone you do not know yet, consider doing a stone casting to get information about this person. This time use your other collection of stones—the ones that represent different types of energy and qualities (see pages 162–163).

Do another stone casting to find out what a particular person feels about you. To do this kind of casting, gather together the stones that represent certain emotions to you and the clear quartz crystal, which represents neutral feelings. Mix the stones together in the bag. Hold the bag while you ask to see what a particular person thinks about you. Put your hand in the bag and pull out one stone only. This stone will indicate whether or not your friend loves you (yet!).

TAROT

The tarot deck is a form of divination which is thought by some to have evolved from ancient Egyptian magical texts. The deck consists of seventy-eight cards, divided into two parts.

The first part is called the Major Arcana and consists of twenty-two cards that are almost self-explanatory, because they are well illustrated and have descriptive titles. The Major Arcana can be used to aid your psychic and spiritual growth during meditation, and/or they can be used for fortune-telling—this involves interpreting their more practical meanings. These cards represent twenty-two aspects of human life.

The second part of the tarot, the Minor Arcana, consists of fifty-six cards divided into four suits. The Cups signify emotional issues and family ties and represent the water signs of Cancer, Pisces, and Scorpio. The Wands signify energy, communications, and social issues and represent the fire signs of Aries, Leo, and Sagittarius. The Pentacles signify material and financial issues and represent the earth signs of Taurus, Virgo, and Capricorn. The Swords signify physical and mental health plus the difficult issues we face in life and represent the air signs of Aquarius, Gemini, and Libra.

Each of the Minor Arcana suits has four court cards and ten numbered cards. The court cards—the King, Queen, Knight, and Page—usually represent people: a dominant male, a dominant female, an ambitious person (the knight), and a youngster (the page). The numbered cards follow a cycle of events, from new beginnings to completion.

When you are a beginning student of tarot, it is best to choose a

simple layout (see pages 168–169) to answer your questions. You
will be surprised how much information is revealed in only twelve
of seventy-eight cards. You can use the same layout over and over to
ask as many questions as you wish. When you become a more
advanced student, you can extend and vary the layout. Eventually,
as a full-fledged master of the craft, you can use as many cards as
you like for a single consultation.

Example: Reading of the Fool

The following pages can cover only the essential meaning of each of
the seventy-eight cards in the tarot deck, as well as the meanings of

each card reversed. However, to help
you understand all there is to see in
each card, and to encourage you to
look for the deeper meanings, here is
one interpretation of the Fool card.

No number has been assigned to
the card of the Fool, because it
represents the innocence and
ignorance of our character as we
enter this world; it is called "0,"
because zero is the degree of
knowledge we are born with—

except for our intuitive skills. Take a good look at the illustration of
the Fool, above. Notice how carefree his general attitude appears to
be: ignorance is bliss for him, for he sees and knows no danger. His
brightly colored clothes represent his carefree attitude.

He carries with him only a white rose (representing purity of
thought) and a wooden staff with a brightly colored bag attached
(representing the bundle of experiences which he will surely
encounter). At his side is a white dog (man's best friend), which
represents his conscience—the only thing he can depend on when
he is alone and has to make his own decisions.

Beautiful butterflies distract his attention (reminding him how
fragile life can be), but the dog appears to be barking already, trying
to tell him to stop and look before he leaps, for there is danger
ahead. He is at the very edge of a steep cliff and will surely fall if
he takes another step in the direction he is going. The choice is
his alone.

HOW TO USE THE TAROT

The tarot cards are potent and deserve respect. Before and after use it is a good idea to carefully wrap your tarot cards in a piece of black or purple velvet cloth, always returning the cards to their upright position so that they are ready for use again.

Spread the complete deck of seventy-eight cards—facedown—on a table with a smooth surface. Mix the cards on the table, making sure they thoroughly intermingle, then collect the entire deck—picture side away from you. Now shuffle the cards the same way you would shuffle ordinary playing cards, but do not flick them. During this process, concentrate on the issue you wish to address.

Layout 1

There are many layouts that can be adopted to help you read the solution to a particular issue. One of the simplest methods is to use the horseshoe spread. If you have a serious question to ask of the tarot cards, use only the Major Arcana cards with this spread.

Once you have shuffled your cards, choose seven cards from the deck and spread them out in the following horseshoe pattern, starting from left to right. Each card represents a particular aspect of your issue.

Use the individual meanings of the cards (see pages 170–171) to find out how to interpret the cards that have revealed themselves.

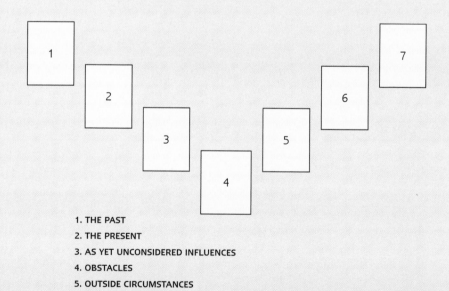

1. THE PAST
2. THE PRESENT
3. AS YET UNCONSIDERED INFLUENCES
4. OBSTACLES
5. OUTSIDE CIRCUMSTANCES
6. BEST SOLUTIONS
7. OUTCOME

Layout 2

Lay out the cards as in the illustration below; interpret them by referring to the individual meanings of the cards on pages 170–177. This layout is an excellent choice for the novice and the expert, because it is an easy question-and-answer method.

Always check the surrounding cards to establish the right context. For example, if you have the Empress in your layout, which represents fertility, pregnancy, motherhood, but also refers to the growth of nature or industry or whatever, you need to check the other cards to see which of these alternatives is relevant to your reading—if the reading is about business, obviously pregnancy is an unlikely interpretation for this card.

Sometimes the cards will seem to be contradicting each other. For instance, you may see the Ace of Cups (a great deal of personal happiness) followed by the Moon (a card of fear, doubt, confusion). Don't be alarmed; you will soon learn to interconnect the meanings. In this particular case the message would be that though you fear disappointment, you need not worry, because the Ace of Cups has already promised happiness and it will deliver—the cards do not lie.

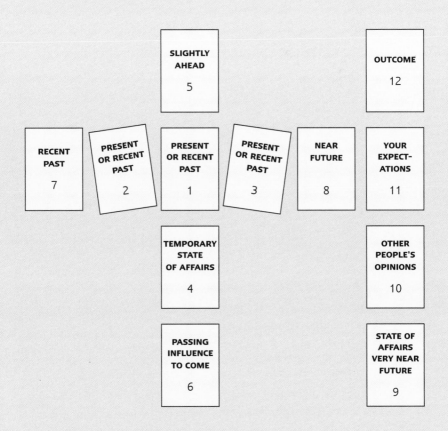

BASIC MEANINGS OF THE MAJOR ARCANA

0 THE FOOL • *Upright:* You are about to embark on a new experience. Don't forget to look before you leap. ***Reversed:*** You are making a habit of repeating the same mistakes over and over.

I THE MAGICIAN • *Upright:* A brilliant person who is a specialist in his or her field. Often associated with the medical profession. ***Reversed:*** The abuse or waste of a superior talent.

II THE HIGH PRIESTESS • *Upright:* A highly intuitive female, capable of great psychic power. ***Reversed:*** Misguided psychic talent.

III THE EMPRESS • *Upright:* Fertility, growth, expansion. Also, this card represents predominantly feminine qualities. ***Reversed:*** Infertility; sometimes a miscarriage; someone confused about his or her sexuality.

IV THE EMPEROR • *Upright:* A well-respected man in a position of power and authority. ***Reversed:*** Abuse of authority; a control freak.

V THE HIGH PRIEST • *Upright:* Conservative, traditional beliefs. Respect for discipline. ***Reversed:*** Unconventional thinking; rebellion against tradition.

VI THE LOVERS • *Upright:* Mutual love; a well-matched couple; also, a card of choice. ***Reversed:*** Confusion about the choices in your love life.

VII THE CHARIOT • *Upright:* A good feeling about having control of your life; also represents a vehicle. ***Reversed:*** Things are out of control in your life; you need self-discipline; also, car accidents.

VIII STRENGTH • *Upright:* Emotional nature; physical and mental strength; you can achieve anything. ***Reversed:*** Weakness of a physical or mental nature.

IX THE HERMIT • *Upright:* "Seek and ye shall find" a material or spiritual object or desire. ***Reversed:*** You feel alone and lost; may also refer to lost property.

X WHEEL OF FORTUNE • *Upright:* The wheel of fortune spins in your favor at this time. ***Reversed:*** Some days you just can't win.

XI JUSTICE • *Upright:* A fair and just outcome to a problem; also represents a well-balanced personality. *Reversed:* An unjust outcome; you are being treated unfairly.

XII THE HANGED MAN • *Upright:* A reversal of fortune—good or bad. *Reversed:* Self-sacrifice and martyrdom.

XIII DEATH • *Upright:* A sudden dramatic change of fortune, totally unexpected. *Reversed:* The slow, drawn-out recovery of a difficult situation.

XIV TEMPERANCE • *Upright:* Things will go well for you—the forces around you are blending together; also refers to good communications. *Reversed:* Turbulence, uneasiness, or bad timing.

XV THE DEVIL • *Upright:* Temptation visits all of us from time to time. Remember, all things in moderation. *Reversed:* Overindulgence and hedonistic behavior. Don't forget, a price has to be paid.

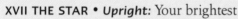

XVI THE TOWER • *Upright:* Sudden catastrophe or danger—don't take risks at this time. *Reversed:* Sometimes you are your own worst enemy—don't indulge in self-destructive behavior.

XVII THE STAR • *Upright:* Your brightest hopes and wishes will be fulfilled and the gods are on your side. *Reversed:* The fulfillment of your hopes and dreams will be delayed, but do not abandon them.

XVIII THE MOON • *Upright:* Fears and phobias are causing you to doubt yourself. *Reversed:* Nervous breakdowns and mental disorders.

XIX THE SUN • *Upright:* Everything is growing and expanding; there are celebrations ahead. *Reversed:* You must wait a little longer to enjoy the fruits of your labor.

XX JUDGMENT • *Upright:* You may be called for jury duty or as a witness. *Reversed:* You will be the victim of poor judgment.

XXI THE WORLD • *Upright:* Reward for completing a task. *Reversed:* Unfinished business.

Finances and the Major Arcana

The tarot is an excellent way to find out what issues are involved in your current financial situation and what elements will come into play to help you get out of your problems or work toward your continued success. Here is a list of the Major Arcana cards specifically tailored for the interpretation of financial matters.

CARD	NAME	MEANING	REVERSAL
0	The Fool	New risky venture	Gambling on the future
1	The Magician	Creative guidance	Denial of guidance
2	The High Priestess	Secrets (your competitive edge)	Concealed or secret enemies
3	The Empress	Growth and abundance	Lack of money
4	The Emperor	Responsibility and leadership	Lack of direction
5	The High Priest	Education	Rebelling against restraints
6	The Lovers	Choice between two paths	Risky new partnership and possible deception
7	The Chariot	Business travel	Lack of direction
8	Strength	Determination	Doubt
9	The Hermit	Good advice	Restlessness
10	The Wheel of Fortune	Sudden good luck	Delays beyond your control
11	Justice	Weighing pros and cons	Injustice and possible legal problems
12	The Hanged Man	Self-sacrifice	Unwillingness to learn
13	Death	Transition	Stagnation
14	Temperance	Teamwork	Disagreements
15	The Devil	Financial concerns	Release from worry
16	The Tower	Upheaval	Inflexibility
17	The Star	Hope	Stress
18	The Moon	Unfounded illusions and confusion	Check details
19	The Sun	Fulfillment and success	Exposure of wrongdoings
20	Judgment	New ideas	Punishment for failure to act
21	The World	Completion and success	Exhaustion, leading to an inability to complete the project

INDIVIDUAL MEANINGS OF CARDS
IN THE MINOR ARCANA
The Cups

Cups represent both good and bad emotional issues, family matters, and love and romance.

ACE • *Upright:* Peace of mind and personal happiness. *Reversed:* Disappointments or disruptive influences.

TWO • *Upright:* Commitment, engagement, or a bond being forged. *Reversed:* Broken promises; broken romance.

THREE • *Upright:* Pregnancy—a welcome addition to the family. *Reversed:* False pregnancy or a miscarriage.

FOUR • *Upright:* Refusal to accept a potential cup of happiness from the hand of fate; fear of disappointment. *Reversed:* Inability to forget past disappointments or a refusal to move on.

FIVE • *Upright:* Worry that love will pass you by; feeling unloved. *Reversed:* You begin to take a chance on love again.

SIX • *Upright:* Love of children; happy memories of childhood. *Reversed:* Constantly living in the past; may also refer to a reunion with long-lost friends or family.

SEVEN • *Upright:* A card of choice: several opportunities present themselves; time to prioritize. *Reversed:* Missed opportunities because of indecision.

EIGHT • *Upright:* Temptation to pursue temporary distractions even though all is well at home. *Reversed:* Putting emotional security at risk, believing the grass to be greener on the other side of the fence.

NINE • *Upright:* Emotional contentment; the satisfaction of knowing your brightest dreams will be fulfilled. *Reversed:* You may be in danger of becoming complacent because all is going so well.

TEN • *Upright:* Ideal family condition: the right partner, healthy children, emotional security. *Reversed:* Disruptions within the family; temporary setbacks that require the family to pull together.

PAGE • *Upright:* This card has a dual meaning: sometimes it represents a new opportunity but it can also represent a female child. *Reversed:* A missed opportunity or a boy child.

KNIGHT • *Upright:* A single young man (water sign) looking for adventure. *Reversed:* This same young man has become fickle and unreliable.

QUEEN • *Upright:* A fair-haired lady, good-natured, kind-hearted, usually married or attached (water sign). *Reversed:* This same lady is now restless, easily bored, looking for excitement.

KING • Upright: A fair-haired, blue-eyed, mature man, good-natured, a hard worker, family-oriented, usually married or attached (water sign). **Reversed:** This same man has now become possessive and overbearing and prone to selfishness.

The Wands

Wands represent communication, energy, the life force, and social issues.

ACE • Upright: Good news; a new beginning; the birth of a baby. **Reversed:** Delays, hassles, or growing pains with new ventures.

TWO • Upright: A person who feels in control of all he or she surveys; a new property owner. **Reversed:** A potentially good property transaction goes wrong.

THREE • Upright: Overseas trading or the achievement of success because of the person's capacity to know a good thing when he or she sees it. **Reversed:** Overzealousness causes rash decisions with overseas trading.

FOUR • Upright: Celebration of security; purchase of a high-rise building; sometimes represents an outdoor wedding. **Reversed:** Postponement of a celebration due to unexpected setbacks.

FIVE • Upright: Arguments, fighting, struggles, and inner turmoil due to misunderstandings. **Reversed:** An explosive situation comes to a head and may result in violent action.

SIX • Upright: Success, triumph, victory, or reward for hard work. **Reversed:** Lack of appreciation or no reward for all a person's efforts.

SEVEN • Upright: Advantage, gain, or success over adversity. **Reversed:** Disadvantage, loss, or a victim of circumstances beyond a person's control.

EIGHT • Upright: Speed, action, or movement. An excellent start may be expected for a new project. **Reversed:** More haste, less speed is an appropriate warning for new ventures.

NINE • Upright: Represents a person who is always guarding and double checking his or her security, but he or she can be assured of safety. **Reversed:** A valid feeling of insecurity.

TEN • Upright: Pressure, stress, or burdens. Carrying a heavy load or problems with excess body fat. **Reversed:** Weight loss and the easing of pressure and stressful situations.

PAGE • Upright: A female child or the start of new but small project. **Reversed:** A male child or short-term delays to new projects.

KNIGHT • *Upright:* A young man (fire sign), unattached, brown hair, hazel eyes, lots of charisma, honest, trustworthy, and fun loving. ***Reversed:*** He is too popular for his own good and has become a lovable rogue.

QUEEN • *Upright:* A mature-minded female, brunette, hazel eyes. Loyal, dependable, good wife and partner, loving, caring mother, but a chatterbox. ***Reversed:*** A jealous, possessive female who tends to gossip a lot but is not vindictive.

KING • *Upright:* A kind, warm-hearted mature man with brown hair and hazel eyes. Down-to-earth, honest, makes an excellent friend for both sexes. He represents a hard worker who loves routine and has a very approachable nature (fire sign). ***Reversed:*** A practical joker, likes attention, flirtatious but not sleazy.

The Pentacles

Pentacles represent the material world, finance, business transactions, and the effect these things have on our lives.

ACE • *Upright:* Financial gain, or a person will find that everything's coming up roses in his or her current material world. ***Reversed:*** Money keeps coming in—but it comes in one door and goes out another.

TWO • *Upright:* Financial turbulence has you juggling the income; you lose some and you win some. ***Reversed:*** No amount of financial wizardry seems to be working for you right now.

THREE • *Upright:* Material recognition and reward for a job well done. ***Reversed:*** You are being underpaid and overworked.

FOUR • *Upright:* This card represents a person who knows the value of money and how to invest it. ***Reversed:*** Represents a miserly approach to finances—it's a good idea to hold on to what you have, but you can't take it with you when you go.

FIVE • *Upright:* Temporary loss of income and a consequential decline in lifestyle and self-respect. ***Reversed:*** Long-term unemployment and loss of income. A person may need assistance from a charitable or welfare society.

SIX • *Upright:* The person will be in a position of being able to assist others financially. ***Reversed:*** The person's generosity will be taken advantage of.

SEVEN • *Upright:* Indicates a slow but steady rise in income. The person can now start a new savings account. ***Reversed:*** The person's meager bank account is constantly being attacked. It's in the bank one day and the next day it's out.

EIGHT • *Upright:* This card represents the apprentice or a new job; we all have to start somewhere. A person will only get out what he puts in. *Reversed:* What seemed like a good opportunity soon collapses; be prepared to try again.

NINE • *Upright:* The luxuries of life are at the person's fingertips; it is a time of opulence; the person can now celebrate the fruits of her labor. *Reversed:* A lack of respect for wealth can lead to hedonistic behavior.

TEN • *Upright:* This card represents a family business, which thrives and ensures that the family fortune remains intact for future generations. *Reversed:* Friction, arguments, or discord over the family fortune may cause it to be lost.

PAGE • *Upright:* A dark-haired, intelligent, female child, or a golden opportunity is recognized and seized upon. *Reversed:* A dark-haired intelligent male child, or a lost opportunity.

KNIGHT • *Upright:* A dark-haired, intelligent, single young man who is down-to-earth, uncomplicated, and focused (earth sign). *Reversed:* He is now arrogant, has tunnel vision, and thinks he's always right.

QUEEN • *Upright:* A dark-haired, mature-minded female, honest and reliable. One who appreciates the material world she lives in (earth sign). *Reversed:* A dark-haired, mature-minded female who is cynical and does not suffer fools gladly (earth sign).

KING • *Upright:* A dark-haired mature man, confident, intelligent, practical, and well respected (earth sign). *Reversed:* A dark-haired mature man, self-righteous, judgmental, and intolerant (earth sign).

The Swords

Swords represent the more serious and difficult issues we face in life. Sometimes life bites back at us and we must deal with it.

ACE • *Upright:* The hand of fate forces a decision that brings victory; success. *Reversed:* Poor decisions—or reluctance to make an important one—prove to be disastrous.

TWO • *Upright:* A truce must be called for a situation that cannot be solved any other way. *Reversed:* Stubbornness; there are none so blind as those who refuse to see.

THREE • *Upright:* Heartache, heartbreak, broken romance (sometimes physical heart problems). *Reversed:* Broken romance; heartache is taking a long time to heal.

THE A-Z OF FORTUNE-TELLING

FOUR • *Upright:* Urgent need for rest, or refers to a hospital bed.
Reversed: Forced confinement.

FIVE • *Upright:* Battle (emotional or physical) fought and won.
Reversed: Battle against adversities fought and lost.

SIX • *Upright:* Serious effort to escape turbulent times for the sake
of peace of mind and a more tranquil environment; also a reference
to refugees. *Reversed:* An unsuccessful attempt to escape difficult
circumstances.

SEVEN • *Upright:* A thief or traitor in the camp goes undetected.
Reversed: The thief or traitor will be caught in the act.

EIGHT • *Upright:* Imprisoned circumstances or a feeling of complete
helplessness. *Reversed:* Breaking away from restrictions and
confinement.

NINE • *Upright:* Migraine headaches; nervous disorders; a
breakdown; deep depression. *Reversed:* Slow recovery from stress
and nervous conditions.

TEN • *Upright:* Physical abuse; backstabbing of the worst kind;
violence. *Reversed:* Slow recovery from the above conditions.

PAGE • *Upright:* A female child who is moody and has a secretive
nature. Can also refer to investigations of a secretive nature and
spying. *Reversed:* A male child who is moody and has a secretive
nature. Can also refer to a sickness that is difficult to diagnose.

KNIGHT • *Upright:* A young man, olive complexion, dark hair, who
loves adventure and speed and who is a risk-taker (air sign).
Reversed: A dark-haired young man who is out of control and
dangerous to himself and others.

QUEEN • *Upright:* A mature female who is accustomed to adversity
and is not afraid to confront difficult issues. She has also been
unlucky in love (air sign). *Reversed:* She has become bitter and
hardened because of repeated letdowns (air sign).

KING • *Upright:* A mature man in a position of authority, a lawyer
or a politician who is confrontational but fair-minded (air sign).
Reversed: He is likely to abuse his position of authority and
become tyrannical.

TEA-LEAF AND COFFEE GROUND READING

Mastering the art of tea-leaf reading not only provides you with skills of insight and divination, but it also creates a pleasant and entertaining pastime with which to impress your friends at the end of a dinner party.

THE CEREMONY

Most readers find that the leaves of China tea form the most easily read pictures, and that it is essential to use a wide-rimmed, plain cup and saucer. Tea-leaf readers prefer to use a round table or form a circle, in the middle of which they place a lit candle or incense burner.

Clients are then invited to sip the tea while thinking of the questions they wish answered. Before the cup is completely drained of liquid, when only the dregs are left, the client takes the cup in the left hand and turns it counterclockwise three times in a full circle, while silently making a wish or asking a question about his or her future.

The cup is then turned upside down onto the saucer and left for a few minutes, so that the leaves can dry out a little. The exercise of transforming the tea leaves into pictures and then into a story is now ready to begin.

The reader takes the cup in the right hand and studies the patterns and pictures from all angles. Do not be alarmed or dismayed if, as a student of the craft, your first viewing appears as nothing more than dense or scattered masses of dried tea leaves— taking the extra time to look for symbols and signs is well worth the effort. Take a few deep breaths and relax; enjoy the atmosphere and you will begin to see the transformation of the leaves into a picture and a story.

Good omens

Acorn, anchor, angel, bee, bird, bouquet, clover, corn, cradle, crown, daffodil, dice, dove, duck, eagle, egg, elephant, fish, flower, fruit, garland, gem, gift, hand, heart, heather, horseshoe, ingot, key, lantern, magician, peacock, queen, rabbit, calm sea, square, star, sun, trophy, trumpet,unicorn

Bad omens

Bat, black flag, cloud, coffin, cross, dagger, gun, monkey, moon, mountain, mouse, owl, rat, raven, scythe, skeleton, skull, snake, sword, tear, teeth, tower, wolf, wreath

Timing

Predicting the timing of events as seen in the tea leaves or coffee grounds is relatively simple if you remember that this method of fortune-telling rarely predicts events beyond twelve months away. The very top and rim of the cup represent the immediate future; the bottom of the cup represents events that will take twelve months to evolve; and the center of the cup represents six months.

USING COFFEE GROUNDS

The procedure for coffee ground readings is virtually the same as for a tea-leaf reading. The only important variation is the preparation of the coffee grounds—you will need to make your cup of coffee by boiling coffee grounds in a saucepan on a stovetop.

To make two cups of coffee, you will need about 3 tablespoons of coffee and 2 cups of water. Bring the water to a boil and measure in the coffee. Allow the mixture to boil for 5 minutes. Experiment with the quantities and timing according to your taste.

Pour the coffee into two white or light-colored coffee cups that are shallow and fairly wide. Do not use a coffee mug or an espresso cup with steep vertical sides. Then follow the same procedures as you would for a tea-leaf reading.

TEA-LEAF READING TIP

When a symbol appears close to the handle of your cup, it means that the predictions related to it will affect you personally. If the symbol is positioned directly opposite the cup handle, the predictions it relates to are to affect someone outside your immediate family.

LIST OF SYMBOLS

Below are some of the regular symbols that appear in tea leaves and coffee grounds:

ACORNS	herald the good news that financial conditions are improving.
ANCHORS	are a sign of good luck and faithfulness in marriage.
ANGELS	seem to appear whenever good tidings are due.
ARROWS	symbolize unwelcome news—something needs urgent attention.
AXES	mean that your troubles will be overcome after some hard work.
BATS	warn you to be aware of false friends.
BEES	represent a virtual hive of enjoyable activity.
BELLS	denote the happy news of a wedding.
BIRDS	are signs of good luck, especially if they are flying.
BOATS	predict the start of a holiday or vacation.
BRIDGES	signify embarking on a successful journey.
CANDLES	show kindness and/or spirituality, especially if they appear to be lit.
CASTLES	denote the fulfillment of high ideals, goals, and expectations.
CHURCHES	represent solemn occasions such as marriages, christenings, or funerals.
CLOUDS	denote disappointment.
CROSSES	predict problems and arguments.
CROWNS	signify the achievement of success.
DAGGERS	predict secret enemies.
DOGS	represent good friends.
DOTS	signify the possibility of more money coming.
DOVES	represent peace of mind and personal happiness.
DRUMS	represent noisy parties; also gossip.
EAGLES	represent a position of authority, in law, government, or politics.
EGGS	that are well formed show good vibrations; cracked or broken, they have bad vibes.
ELEPHANTS	show good fortune: soon if the trunk is up, later if it is down.
EYES	warn you that you must watch out for unexpected problems or delays.
FEATHERS	represent fragility regarding a physical or mental condition.
FENCES	suggest that you are imprisoned by your personal circumstances.
FISH	signify that you will experience a bounteous catch.
FLIES	represent minor setbacks.
GARLANDS	represent honors that will be bestowed upon you.

GLASSES	suggest that you are vulnerable to lies and deception; also, they suggest false friends.
GUNS	mean that someone is "gunning" for you (not literally).
HAMMERS	signify that you will succeed after some hard work.
HARPS	show that your lifestyle is or will be of a high standard.
HEARTS	mean love, romance, marriage, and happy results in emotional issues.
HOUSES	signify that your work and home are on stable ground.
JESTERS	are practical jokers; they suggest frivolous actions.
JOCKEYS	tell you to take a chance, place a bet, because you are going to be lucky; a winning streak.
KEYS	mean a new experience; new doors open for you with pleasant surprises.
KITES	tell you that you will rise through the ranks to a lofty position.
LAMPS	suggest that you will achieve a deeper understanding of your karmic lessons.
LINES	signify difficulties and hardship if wavy, success if they are straight.
LOGS	are a heavy burden; they also represent stubbornness.
MASKS	mean you will be the victim of deception.
MOON	full means a love affair; half represents marriage for material gain; crescent signifies a new romance.
NUMBERS	could be your lucky lottery numbers.
OWLS	are not good signs; contrary to popular belief, they signify sickness.
PARCELS	suggest a luxurious lifestyle or vanity.
RABBITS	represent timidity, phobias, and fears.
RAINBOWS	mean protection and the assurance of a secure future.
SCALES	are dealings with the law that have a favorable outcome.
SHIPS	mean that at last your ship comes in; an abundance of good luck.
STARS	signify good fortune and harmony.
TABLES	mean a social gathering, a culinary feast.
TREES	represent prosperity, growth, and expansion.
TRIANGLES	signify some unexpected good luck.
UMBRELLAS	reassure you that you will be sheltered from adverse conditions.
VULTURES	warn that you will be the victim of envy and vulnerable to attack.
WAGONS	mean transportation; you will purchase a new vehicle.
WINDMILLS	mean that slowly but surely you will achieve success.
WINGS	refer to a messenger who will bring good news.

WAX READING

Dropping various objects or substances into water and examining
the shapes and symbols that form in the water is an ancient
technique of divination. Over the centuries, the effect of water on
various things, ranging from barley cakes (alphitomancy) to wax
to lead, has been explored and documented. All these types of
divination work on the same principle, but each has a different level
of complexity in terms of the preparation of the media.

Wax reading is one of the least complicated and time-consuming
of these forms of divination. While it is not dangerous, it should
still be undertaken with extreme care; it is wise to enlist the services
of—or work with—a psychic who specializes in this craft.

It is best to carry out this procedure during a full moon. Fill a
clean shallow bowl almost full of fresh, clean water, preferably from
a clear, bubbling stream or a lake. Do not use salt water. Leave the
water in the bowl overnight, in a position where the water will
reflect the moonlight.

The next day, set up your bowl in the middle of your special
psychic space (see pages 52–61) and bring some matches and a fat,
natural-colored (if you are using a clear or silver colored bowl) or
white (if you are using a colored bowl) beeswax candle.

Sit in front of the bowl. First, focus on your breathing, then
allow your mind to still (see pages 18–23 for a more detailed
description of some meditation techniques). When you feel ready,
light the candle, half close your eyes, and ask your question about
the future. Let the wax pool on the top of the candle before
carefully pouring it into the water.

If you have asked about the name of your future lover, you may
find that the first drop into the water will form a letter—this will
usually be the first letter of that person's name.

Keep a journal, and before you light the candle, write down the
question you are going to ask. As soon as the wax shape has formed
in the water, note down the first image, impression, or idea you

receive upon looking at the shape in the water. The wax may seem completely shapeless, but it will trigger a response if your mind is ready to receive it.

Place the candle on a wide porcelain or earthenware dish as you write your impressions in your journal. Continue pouring the wax into the water until you feel that you have received a complete answer to your question.

LEAD READING

This unusual method of fortune-telling requires great skill. It is a highly potent technique, practiced by only a few psychics who claim it as their specialty and who guard the craft with great secrecy. Though lead reading is reputed to be a very accurate method of fortune-telling, it is by no means the most popular.

The process is very time-consuming. First the lead is melted down. While it is still hot, it is ladled into a tub of cold water. This causes the lead to form various shapes and symbols, which are interpreted by the psychic as predictions.

Caution: There is extreme risk in handling hot lead. It should not be undertaken by anyone but an experienced practitioner.

AFFIRMATION Also known as positive affirmation, this is a concise statement describing a personal goal or wish.

AMULET A protective device worn around the neck or hung from the door or window of a sacred space or home. The terms "amulets," "charms," and "talismans" tend to be used interchangeably.

ASTROLOGY A form of divination based on the position of the planets, moon, and sun at the time of a person's birth.

AURA A form of psychic energy expressed as layers of rainbowlike colors that surround the physical body; they range in depth and form, depending on a person's emotional and physical state.

CHARM A magical word or words that can be used as a protection.

CHINESE HOROSCOPE A form of divination based on the particular year in which you were born.

CIRCLE A sacred space, usually thought of as a sphere of energy created when the circle is cast, which is done by imagining a blue line of energy separating the everyday world from a person's safe space "between the worlds."

CLAIRAUDIENCE The ability to hear words, sentences, or names transmitted from the spirit world or your higher self.

CLAIRVOYANCE The ability to visualize images, situations, or symbols transmitted from the spirit world or your higher self.

CREATIVE VISUALIZATION An active meditation in which we focus on images or feelings in order to move beyond our limitations and current beliefs.

DIVINATION A catchall phrase used to refer to the myriad techniques of trying to foretell the future by interpreting signs, visions, images, or patterns seen in the stars (astrology), numbers (numerology), cards (tarot and playing cards), dice, water (water scrivening), the lines on a person's palm (palmistry), stones (stone casting), or tea leaves or coffee grounds (hydromancy).

EXTRASENSORY PERCEPTION (ESP) This is often called the sixth sense.

GROUNDING Connecting the body's energy to that of the earth.

GUARDIAN ANGEL An energy form that is devoted to helping guide you through life by increasing your awareness of your higher self.

INTUITION Another word for nonintellectual reasoning: the ability to receive energy in the form of feelings or "vibes" that cause you to "know" something significant about a person, event, or place.

INVOKE To summon a spirit or energy form into oneself.

MEDITATION A relaxation or spiritual technique used to help you still your mind so that you can tap into your higher self or a higher consciousness.

NUMEROLOGY A form of divination using numbers to learn about your personality and path in life.

PALMISTRY Otherwise known as chiromancy, palmistry is a form of divination based on the lines of a person's palm and the shape of a person's hand and fingers.

PENDULUM A stone or metal weight that is tied to the end of a piece of string or a length of chain. Most New Age stores stock pendulums. However, you can easily make one for yourself. All you need to do is find a smallish, tear-shaped piece of metal or stone (such as an amethyst, a quartz crystal, or a faceted piece of lead crystal) that has a point at the bottom. Drill a hole at the top and thread a length of chain, string, or even horsehair through it. It is important that the pendulum swings freely from its chain or string. The stone or metal pendulum must be heavy enough to keep some tension along the line.

PSYCHIC A person who is able to accurately predict world or local events or see into the secrets and intimate experiences of people they have never met before.

PSYCHIC CIRCLE See "Circle."

PSYCHIC SHIELDS Psychic forms of protection that help screen a person from many forms of negative energy.

PSYCHIC SPACE A special area that you set aside for practicing and developing your psychic abilities.

PSYCHIC WORK Any concentrated form of psychic activity that involves the intuition, including fortune-telling and spell craft.

PSYCHIC WORKSHOPS Places of learning that help students develop their psychic abilities.

PSYCHOMETRY The ability to psychically derive information about a person from his or her personal property, such as jewelry or clothing.

RUNES Magical symbols that were first used by ancient Nordic and Germanic cultures and are still used for divination.

SCRIVENING A form of divination using reflective surfaces, such as a crystal ball, water, ice, mirrors, or smoke from a fire.

SCRYING see "Scrivening."

SPELL CRAFT A technique used to cast spells for a particular purpose or to find an answer to a particular question.

SPIRIT GUIDE An energy form that can help guide a person toward a state of higher consciousness.

STONE CASTING A form of divination where semiprecious or precious stones are used to reveal the future.

TALISMAN An object charged to attract a specific magical energy. The most popular talismans correspond with a particular celestial body and should be made on the day of the week that resonates with that celestial body. The table below shows some relevant correspondences:

DAY OF THE WEEK	CELESTIAL BODY	CORRESPONDING ENERGY
Monday	Moon	Psychic ability
Tuesday	Mars	Honor and courage
Wednesday	Mercury	Eloquence and protection
Thursday	Jupiter	Riches and health
Friday	Venus	Love and travel
Saturday	Saturn	Business and learning
Sunday	Sun	Wealth and friends

TAROT A deck of specially designed cards that are used as a form of divination. The deck contains 78 cards and is divided into the Major Arcana of 22 cards and the Minor Arcana of 56 cards. The Minor Arcana is further divided into four groups, representing the four elements of earth, air, fire, and water.

TELEPATHY The ability to deliberately send thoughts to and/or receive thoughts from a person.

UNIVERSAL SUBCONSCIOUS A form of higher energy believed to contain the sum of our innate knowledge.

WAX READING A technique for reading the future from the shapes and symbols that form when hot wax is slowly dripped into a bowl of water.

ZODIAC A collective term referring to the twelve astrological signs: Aries, Taurus, Gemini, Cancer, Leo, Virgo, Libra, Scorpio, Sagittarius, Capricorn, Aquarius, and Pisces.

SUGGESTED READING

M. and A. Adams. *The Learned Arts of Witches & Wizards: History and Traditions of White Magic*. Sydney: Lansdowne Publishing, 1998.

——. *The World of Wizards: Modern Magical Tools and Ancient Traditions*. Sydney: Lansdowne Publishing, 2002.

A. Beattie. *Love Magic*. Sydney: Lansdowne Publishing, 1999.

——. *Money Magic*. Sydney: Lansdowne Publishing, 2000.

——. *The Girls' Handbook of Spells*. Sydney: Lansdowne Publishing, 2000.

——. *The Feng Shui Guide to Clearing Your Space*. Sydney: Lansdowne Publishing, 2000.

——. *Astrology Dictionary*. Sydney: Lansdowne Publishing, 2003.

A. Beattie and A. Wolf. *The Girls' Guide to Spells*. Sydney: Lansdowne Publishing, 2001.

P. Beyerl. *The Master Book of Herbalism*. Washington, D.C.: Phoenix Publishing, 1984.

S. Cunningham. *Cunningham's Encyclopedia of Crystal, Gem & Metal Magic*. St. Paul, MN: Llewellyn, 1997.

——. *Cunningham's Encyclopedia of Magical Herbs*. St. Paul, MN: Llewellyn, 1990.

——. *Earth, Air, Fire and Water*. St. Paul, MN: Llewellyn, 1992.

——. *Magical Herbalism*. St. Paul, MN: Llewellyn, 1989.

N. Drury. *Creative Visualization*. Sydney: Lansdowne Publishing, 2001.

S. Ducie. *Thorsons Principles of Numerology*. London: Thorsons, 1998.

P. Fenton-Smith. *Astrology Revealed*. Sydney: Simon & Schuster, 1997.

——. *Palmistry Revealed*. Sydney: Simon & Schuster, 1996.

——. *The Tarot Revealed*. Sydney: Simon & Schuster, 1995.

P. Glass-Koentop. *The Magic in Stones*. St. Paul, MN: Llewellyn, 1989.

R. Loader. *Dreamstones: Magic from the Living Earth*. Dorset: Prism Press, 1990.

D. and J. Parker. *The Power of Magic: Secrets and Mysteries Ancient and Modern*. London: Mitchell Beazley, 1992.

J. Purser. *Meditation*. Sydney: Lansdowne Publishing, 2000.

E. Thorsson. *A Handbook of Rune Magic*. York Beach, ME: Samuel Weiser, 1984.

C. Walker. *The Encyclopedia of Secret Knowledge*. London: Rider Books, 1995.

H. Whitaker. *Develop Your Psychic Ability*. Sydney: Lansdowne Publishing, 1998.

——. *Fortune Telling*. Sydney: Lansdowne Publishing, 1999.

——. *Palmistry*. Sydney: Lansdowne Publishing, 1998.

——. *Numerology*. Sydney: Lansdowne Publishing, 1997.

H. Whitaker and C. Blanche. *Guardian Angels*. Sydney: Lansdowne Publishing, 1999.

INDEX

Thunder Bay Press
An imprint of the Advantage Publishers Group
5880 Oberlin Drive, San Diego, CA 92121-4794
www.thunderbaybooks.com

All notations of errors or omissions should be addressed to Thunder Bay Press,
Editorial Department, at the above address. All other correspondence (author
inquiries, permissions) concerning the content of this book should be addressed
to Lansdowne Publishing, Level 1, 18 Argyle Street, The Rocks NSW 2000,
Australia.

ISBN 1-59223-032-6
Library of Congress Cataloging-in-Publication Data available on request.

Set in Birka and LT Ergo on QuarkXPress
Printed in Singapore by Tien Wah Press (Pte) Ltd
1 2 3 4 5   07 06 05 04 03

With grateful acknowledgment to Hazel Whitaker for reproduction of a portion
of her work from *Develop Your Psychic Ability*, *Fortune Telling*, *Guardian Angels*,
Numerology and *Palmistry*; to Nevill Drury for reproduction of a portion of his
work *Creative Visualization*; and to Jan Purser for reproduction of a portion of
her work *Meditation*.